A Guide to the Industrial Archeology of Boston Proper

A detail of Mill Creek. From the Bonner Map (1722), courtesy of the
Massachusetts Historical Society.

A Guide to the Industrial Archeology of Boston Proper

Peter Stott

The MIT Press
Cambridge, Massachusetts

This guide, which will form part of *A Guide to the Industrial Archeology of Eastern Massachusetts: Middlesex, Norfolk, and Suffolk Counties*, was prepared on the occasion of the thirteenth annual conference of the Society for Industrial Archeology, Boston, June 14–17, 1984. The full edition of the *Guide* will be published in 1985 by The MIT Press.

This book was set in Baskerville by The MIT Press Computergraphics Department and was printed and bound in the United States of America.

Library of Congress Cataloging in Publication Data

Stott, Peter.
    A guide to the industrial archeology of Boston proper.

    "Will form part of A Guide to the industrial archeology of eastern Massachusetts—Middlesex, Norfolk, and Suffolk counties, . . . prepared on the occasion of the Thirteenth annual Conference of the Society for Industrial Archeology, Boston, June 14–17, 1984, . . . will be published in 1985 by The MIT Press"—Verso of t.p.
    Bibliography: p.
    Includes indexes.
    1. Industrial archaeology—Massachusetts—Boston. I. Society for Industrial Archeology. Conference (13th: 1984: Boston, Mass.) II. Title.
T22.5.B67S76   1984   609'.744'61   84–9643
ISBN 0-262-69090-X (pbk.)

Contents

Preface to the Interim Edition

Landmarks of Industrial Archeology

The terrain of the nation's industrial history is comprised of a large number of greater or lesser features scattered over a broad landscape. To describe this topography, historians have traditionally identified the principal events and tied them together in a common framework of themes. Mapmakers call this process "triangulation"—a technique for accurately mapping the landscape through a series of imaginary triangles whose vertices are high peaks, church steeples, or other prominent landmarks. (By precisely measuring the distance between two points and the observed angles to a third, the distance to the third can be determined.) The larger the number of landmarks, the more accurate the map.

Most of the major landmarks of industrial history, such as the introduction of the water-driven spinning frame or of interchangeable parts, are well documented by historians, establishing, in effect, a national "map" of technological innovation. The record is much less complete, however, at the state and local levels. Too often deductions about the nature of technological innovation have been made without the benefit of an adequate "secondary triangulation," a second generation of more closely spaced triangles, designed to produce large-scale maps of a particular community or region. As a consequence, major portions of these large-scale maps are blank or imperfectly understood. For example, Goodyear's discovery of the vulcanization of rubber in Woburn is well chronicled, but little serious work has been done to trace the line that runs from that discovery to the origins of the industry in the rubber craze of the early 1830s. Again, outside of Reading, Massachusetts, who today remembers that the town was once dominated by the manufacture of pipe organs and organ pipes? Every community has a unique and characteristic economic history, the landmarks of which are important to the construction of a complete record of technological innovation. The present guidebook is an attempt to construct such a secondary triangulation for industrial history. Like any such effort, it is designed as much to create a contemporary record as to provide a network into which future discoveries can be easily fit.

The intangible landmarks of economic history are mirrored in the physical world by the surviving objects and structures associated with them. The Boston Stone is both an artifact of the early paint industry and evidence of early industrial activity in the vicinity of Mill Creek. Its subsequent use as a surveyor's landmark and point of reference for local shops has given the stone a prominence that is unusual for industrial remains. Today most of the surviving physical evidence of 19th-century economic history is as invisible as the intangible history it represents. A small brick building near the Allston Depot was the earliest power station of the nation's largest electrified street railway system. An unmarked pumping station near the old boundary between Hyde Park and Roxbury is the most visible monument to the verbal battles fought over Hyde Park's water supply and the town's annexation to Boston in 1912. A new appreciation for the varied structures of each community will make them stand out in relief against the background of our built environment and illuminate the common threads that bind them.

Industrial archeology is an attempt to study the history of industry and engineering through an examination of their surviving artifacts. From these artifacts we can learn as much about the development of 19th-century economic life as we can about the technological processes on which that life was built and the men and women who made them run. Of necessity, the present work leaves unexamined the large body of resources that exists *below* ground, but it does hint at the wealth of written and artifactual evidence that still remains to be explored.

Technological Innovation in the Boston Area

One way of measuring the industrial vitality of a region is to examine the variety and sources of its innovation—both in new concerns organized and in new processes within established industries. In this respect, eastern Massachusetts seems unusually rich. At various stages in its history, imported technologies, usually from Europe, have provided a stimulus for innovations by local craftsmen, mechanics, entrepreneurs, and engineers. As early as the 17th century, Boston's location on the eastern seaboard gave the community an advantage over other North American towns, and Boston became an important transfer point for both commerce and technology. The introduction of the iron industry at Saugus and its subsequent diffusion throughout the country were paralleled by innovations in other industries in the late 18th and early 19th centuries. By 1850 a group of planned industrial cities were emerging, creating new societal problems that the state's governmental and private agencies were among the first in the country to address. In many cases their solutions were borrowed initially from European practice. The evolution of an urban infrastructure—of water, sewage, transit, and other facilities—can likewise be traced to the needs of an industrial society dependent on organized public services for its growth. In the 20th century, to the extent that manufacturing declined first in the region's older towns and cities, these communities have also been among the first to be revitalized in a "postindustrial" tourist and service economy.

The transfer of technology from Europe, particularly England, was most visible in the early years of the Republic, when the country was most dependent on foreign expertise. "Internal improvements" provided training for many of the nation's first engineers, and they usually benefited from prior European examples. The English engineer William Weston laid out the Middlesex Canal, which was completed under the direction of the "father of American civil engineering," Loammi Baldwin. The opening of the Charles River Bridge between Boston and Charlestown in 1786—the first long-span structure in the New World—provided an important stimulus to other New England bridge builders.

Nowhere was European technology more in evidence than in textile manufacturing, the first factory industry to be established in New England. The machine designs introduced in Pawtucket, Waltham, Taunton, Lowell, and elsewhere were tinkered with and improved on by countless mechanics in the machine shops established in the new textile mills. The range of these shops expanded in the 1820s, and they attracted new apprentices from farms and local blacksmith shops. In the same period, the growth of two parallel industries—granite in Quincy and ice in Cambridge—led to the introduction of innovative materials-handling equipment. Thus, in the period prior to 1830, the Boston area was already developing an important and varied machine industry that would remain an innovative force well into the 20th century.

The liberal reform movement was a response to the problems that grew out of the nation's first planned industrial communities. In 1837 Massachusetts became the first state to collect systematic industrial and employment statistics. In education, the liberal improvements initiated by Horace Mann and the nation's first State Board of Education were expanded after the Civil War with new facilities for technical and scientific training, including the Massachusetts Institute of Technology and the Lawrence Scientific School at Harvard. The creation of the first permanent State Board of Health, established in 1869, encouraged the analysis and expansion of water and sewage systems across the Commonwealth. As early as the late 18th century, Massachusetts towns had taken the lead in the formation of private water companies. After the Civil War, civil engineers were increasingly called upon to design and construct local pumped water-supply systems. Following London's model, Boston developed the nation's first large system of intercepting sewers, completing in the same decade an expansion of its already extensive water-supply system. Under the guidance of the State Board of Health, the Boston area became the first region to address the problems of water supply and sewage disposal as metropolitan issues. Following the lead of European park systems, Frederick Law Olmsted and Charles Eliot established Boston and metropolitan park systems that became a national model. Boston's extensive street-railway network was the first large system to be electrified, and the rapid growth of its traffic in the early 1890s led to the construction of the first streetcar subway in North America.

This brief catalogue sketches only the bare outlines of a pattern of technological and social innovation which, like the successive waves of foreign immigration, reached Boston first before moving west to other parts of the country. By the late 19th century, many areas of innovation that had once been centered in the Boston area or New England—bridge construction and metallurgy, for instance—came to be concentrated in the Midwest.

Although Boston, Cambridge, and other large communities continued to expand in population and overall value of manufactured products into the 1920s, key manufacturing industries such as textiles, shoes, and furniture were already on the decline by the end of the First World War. The Depression merely accelerated this process. Boston's financial and maritime role was usurped by New York, and construction of all kinds declined precipitously. Increasingly, service industries characterized local economies. The relatively recent economic recovery from this position has been due in large part to the strength of the region's educational institutions, particularly in engineering and the applied sciences, which has made possible the modern high-technology industries.

The "postindustrial" economy has also led to the growth of tourism as an industry and to a new appreciation for industrial archeology, manifested in the establishment of federal and state urban cultural parks focused on workplaces that half a century ago frequently were viewed as drear prisons of economic necessity.

About the Interim Edition

This publication, produced to coincide with the thirteenth annual conference of the Society for Industrial Archeology, represents only a small part of a much larger work to be published in 1985 by The MIT Press covering the three Boston-area counties of Middlesex, Norfolk, and Suffolk. "Boston Proper" (a cartographer's term for the original Shawmut Peninsula and the filled land around it) is only one of nine sections of Boston to be surveyed, and one of 94 sections covering the 86 towns and cities of the three counties. Approximately one thousand sites will be described in the final work.

This survey project represents the fortuitous confluence of federal and state initiatives. In its catalogue aspects, the publication is an outgrowth of a decade-old program of the Historic American Engineering Record, an agency of the National Park Service, to identify sites and structures that are significant for the history of industry and engineering. What has made possible the more comprehensive and descriptive approach of this project is the Cultural Resources Reconnaissance Survey, an innovative program begun by the Massachusetts Historical Commission four and a half years ago.

The reconnaissance survey was designed to identify the general development and types of historic resources in each community in the state; since the fall of 1979, nearly 300 of the state's 351 communities have been studied. As a by-product, the survey generated the three-county list of approximately 1,000 sites that forms the basis of the current project. Equally important to this guide, however, is the background material that the survey has generated on the economic development of each town and city. This material has made possible the "gazetteer" format, modeled on the 19th-century works of John Warner Barber, John Hayward, and others.

This publication is jointly sponsored by the Massachusetts Historical Commission, the Historic American Engineering Record, the Charles River Museum of Industry in Waltham, and the Society for Industrial Archeology's Southern New England Chapter, host of the 1984 conference.

Primary criteria for inclusion in the guide consist of the survival of some physical evidence of the industry and a construction date prior to 1940. Structures represented will range over nearly three centuries: from the excavated remains of the 1646 "Braintree" iron furnace in Quincy to Boston Edison's 1940 Mystic Generating Station in Everett. Factories of the shoe industry in Stoneham, Marlborough, Weymouth, and elsewhere will be represented, as will the textile mills of Lowell and the confectionery factories of Cambridge. Bridges, water-supply systems, and railroad structures will also be included. In some structural categories, additional criteria are being employed. In the case of bridges, although an attempt has been made to include all stone-arch bridges, iron and steel girder bridges have not been included regardless of their date; metal truss bridges generally have been limited to ones that are pin-connected (prior to about 1900), and reinforced concrete bridges to those constructed prior to about 1909. As a general rule, wharves, warehouses, and other structures related more to commerce than to manufacturing will be omitted.

The initial lists, culled from a close examination of available contemporary and historic maps and atlases and from insurance surveys, have been compared to secondary histories of each of the communities. The resultant lists were checked against surviving structures and inventory lists compiled by local historical commissions and other agencies. The primary identification of a structure, however, is through atlases and secondary sources. Neither source ever provides a "complete" list, and omissions, particularly of the smallest manufacturers, are inevitable.

The name cited is generally the one associated with the initial construction and operation of the structure. The information in the upper right-hand corner of each entry includes the name of the relevant U.S. Geological Survey topographic map and the coordinates of the site on that map. The entries are cross-referenced by site entry number within the text. The reference **000** refers to entries outside of Boston Proper that will be included in the final edition. Source material consulted in the preparation of each of the entries is included at the end of the book, arranged numerically by entry number. Not cited, because of their constant use, are city and town street directories, contemporary maps and atlases, death certificates from the Bureau of Vital Records and Statistics, state and federal census records, and, for the city of Boston, building permits. Building inventory forms filed by local historical commissions with the Massachusetts Historical Commission have been credited to the name of the compiler.

Acknowledgments

Many individuals and organizations have participated in this project. Among the sponsoring institutions, the Massachusetts Historical Commission has provided the bulk of the financial and staff support without which the project could not have gone forward. I am particularly indebted to the past and present directors of the commission, Patricia Weslowski and Valerie Talmage. The guide's origin in the Cultural Resources Reconnaissance Survey made the commission the book's natural sponsor, and its continuing support has demonstrated its long-term interest in the identification of historic industrial resources. Important research and financial support has come from the Charles River Museum of Industry in Waltham, while the Historic American Engineering Record has provided large-format record photographs for many of the structures in the three-county area. Numerous members of the Southern New England Chapter of the Society for Industrial Archeology have given generously of their time. Much of this help, where it relates to specific entries, I have tried to credit in the notes, though a much more complete acknowledgment will appear in the final edition.

Additional financial support has also been generously granted by the Louis L. Stott Foundation. Grants from the Polaroid Foundation and H. P. Hood, Inc., demonstrated an early and gratifying interest in the project by the private sector.

In the field, many other individuals and local historical commissions and societies made "local inquiry" an invariably pleasant and rewarding experience. Their enthusiasm and that of many industry officials provided a welcome tonic to a sometimes daunted and flagging spirit. This help will also be acknowledged in the notes of the final edition.

Any project of this kind must depend heavily on the support of local libraries and other research institutions. In this respect, the Boston area is well provided. Many local libraries have compiled card indexes to local newspapers which have made the research there especially fruitful. Special thanks should go to the staff of the Boston Athenaeum, the research divisions of the Boston Public Library, the Insurance Library Association of Boston, and MIT's Barker Engineering Library. The libraries of both the Merrimack Valley Textile Museum and the Society for the Preservation of New England Antiquities provided important insurance and advertising illustrations. The credit ledgers of R. G. Dun & Company in the Manuscripts Department at Harvard's Baker Library provided wonderfully informal glimpses of the business activities of many 19th-century firms, supplemented by the department's extensive collection of insurance surveys. Above all, the Massachusetts State Library has provided an unofficial home and office. Its staff and that of its neighbor, the State Archives (a sister agency to the Massachusetts Historical Commission), responded to all of my requests with good humor and allowed me a degree of access to the collections without which it is unlikely the project would have been completed before the end of the century.

Numerous friends and colleagues have read portions of the text, offered comments and suggestions, put up with my questions, and showed great patience when it must have seemed I could talk of nothing else. For this patience I am greatly indebted. I owe a special debt of gratitude to three members of the project's review committee—Eric DeLony, Michael Folsom, and Robert Vogel—who were given the onerous task of reviewing the entire text. Larry Cohen, Science Editor at The MIT Press, has supplied encouragement, advice, and help at all the right moments.

Finally, words cannot express my debt of gratitude to my family, whose patience and support (both moral and financial) provided a refuge from the frustrations of research and writing. To them I dedicate this work.

1 The Boston Stone (**501**), a sketch by George R. Tolman for Edward G. Porter's *Rambles in Old Boston* (1887).

CABINET CUSTOM WORK DEPARTMENT,
At Paine's Manufactory,
48 CANAL, and 141 FRIEND STS., BOSTON,

2 Paine Furniture Company (**502**), from an advertisement, c.1890. Courtesy of the Society for the Preservation of New England Antiquities.

3 Richards Building (**505**), c. 1872. The Atlantic Works had an office in the building between 1870 and 1873. Courtesy of the Bostonian Society.

4 The Boston Post Building (**506**), c. 1895. Walter C. Brooks & Co., merchant
tailors, occupied the first floor of the building from about 1891 until 1904, when
they moved to they newly completed Old South Building nearby. Courtesy of the
Boston Athenaeum.

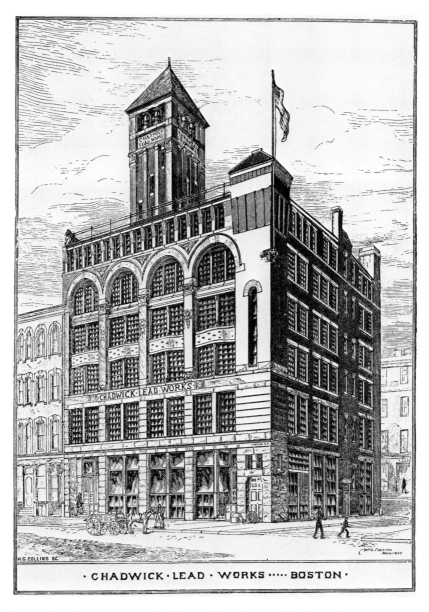

· CHADWICK · LEAD · WORKS ····· BOSTON ·

5 Architect's rendering of the Chadwick Leadworks (**511**), from Charles S. Damrell's *A Half Century of Boston's Building* (1895).

6 An early view of the footbridge (**512**) in the Public Garden and two predecessors of the Swan Boats. Courtesy of the Boston Athenaeum.

7 John J. McNutt's Novelty Woodworks (**518**), from an advertisement in the 1896 *Boston City Directory*. The engraving or a similar view was used in McNutt's advertisements as early as 1864.

8 Varnishing room on the top floor of the Chickering Piano Factory (**525**), 1859. From *Frank Leslie's Illustrated Newspaper*, 7 April 1859, courtesy of the Boston Athenaeum.

9 A trade-card depiction of the Smith-American Organ Company Factory (**526**) prior to the fire that destroyed the mansard roof in 1885. Courtesy of the Society for the Preservation of New England Antiquities.

10 Interior view of the West End Street Railway's Central Power Station (**533**). The triple-expansion steam engines in the foreground powered the generators on the right through a complicated system of belts and pulleys beneath the floor. From the *Street Railway Journal*, September 1892.

11 Subway construction (**534**) at Park Street, November 1896. Surface cars are running on a temporary track over the roof of the subway. From the *Third Annual Report of the Boston Transit Commission*.

12 Construction of the Edison Electric Illuminating Company's Salem Street Station (**546**), 11 June 1909. Courtesy of Boston Edison Company Archives, Allston.

13 A southwest view of the present Boston Light (**555**), six years after its construction in 1783. From *The Massachusetts Magazine*, February 1789, courtesy of the
Boston Athenaeum.

14 Deer Island Pumping Station (**561**), architect's rendering. Left to right: screen house, coal house, boiler room, and engine room. Courtesy of the Library of the Metropolitan District Commission.

Boston Proper

Boston was established in 1630 with the first settlement of the Massachusetts Bay Colony under Governor John Winthrop. Its earliest population, numbering only about 1,000 individuals, occupied a small part of the Shawmut Peninsula, a narrow irregular promontory thrusting out into the middle of Boston Harbor. Almost completely surrounded by water and mudflats, it was linked to the mainland (Roxbury) by a narrow "neck" of land, the route of the present Washington Street through what is today the South End. The town's earliest development occurred in the North End, along Town Cove, and westward along the road to Roxbury. Not until after the Revolution did Boston begin to expand from the narrow peninsula, extending bridges across the water to Charlestown, Cambridge, Roxbury, and South Boston and filling in the various coves and bays by which the town was surrounded. By 1912 landfill operations had expanded the original peninsula from an area of some 780 acres to over 1,900 acres.

Though surrounded by industrial districts later annexed to the city, Boston Proper developed little of the heavy industry characteristic of other parts of the present city. Instead, its early maritime commerce and political position made it a focus of trade and of professional and legal services, which tended to push manufacturing industries to the fringes of the original community. Nevertheless, early town merchants took advantage of the peninsula's shallow coves to create a tidal millpond out of the North Cove (now Haymarket Square), utilizing a 2,000-foot dam connecting the north and west ends of the town. Boston's earliest mills were established on its outlet into Town Cove beginning in 1643. Mill Creek (now Blackstone Street) survived nearly two hundred years, and in the last two decades of its life it served as the southern terminus of the Middlesex Canal, when that waterway was extended across the Charles River, through the Mill Pond and Mill Creek, to docks in Town Cove.

From the start, by virtue of its housing the governor's residence, the monthly courts, and a superior harbor, the town became the center of economic life of the colony and the region. Boston's extensive maritime commerce, upon which the colony depended after large-scale emigration from England ceased in the 1640s, stimulated numerous industries, especially shipbuilding and the manufacture of rope and rum. The West Indies consumed large quantities of New England lumber, fish, cattle, and other produce and offered molasses in exchange. By the 1680s Boston had become the leading port and the largest town in the American colonies, a position she retained for nearly 60 years. Boston's prosperity culminated in the early 18th century with the construction of Long Wharf, extending State Street nearly 2,000 feet into deep water, and Boston Light, the first lighthouse in North America.

By the mid-18th century two smallpox epidemics, the Molasses Act of 1734, and widespread inflation had caused a sharp falloff in trade. Shipbuilding and distilling declined sharply. Boston's population fell as workmen left for country towns. With the passage of successive revenue taxes in the 1760s and 1770s, and with the tightening of customs controls on smuggling, foreign trade (both legal and illegal) was further limited. The colonial period was brought to an end by the political and military expression of the mercantile revolt to these measures.

After the war, Boston merchants looked inland as nascent rural industries began to produce goods to which they could apply their marketing skills. New bridges strengthened Boston's economic ties to the mainland, and increasing quantities of building materials, produce, boots, and shoes were sent to Boston in exchange for European goods, South American hides, furs, and other imports. After 1804, Middlesex Canal boats unloaded lumber, granite, and other products from New Hampshire and northern Middlesex County in the Dock Square area.

The period following the War of 1812 was one of great commercial vitality for Boston, in large part fueled by the prosperous China trade, that had begun in the 1790s. Shipbuilding, already benefiting from the demand for East Indiamen, was further stimulated by tonnage duties imposed by the first U.S. tariff on British-built ships (1789). Between 1810 and 1830, Boston's population doubled. From the towns of northern New England, carpenters, blacksmiths, craftsmen, and mechanics of all sorts made their way to the city. A carriagemaker from Newburyport became an inventor of milling machines; a New Hampshire cabinetmaker became the leading piano manufacturer of his day; a blacksmith from Maine established the first architectural iron foundry in Boston; and hundreds of carpenters and housewrights came to Boston to build her merchant fleet or, later, to erect row after row of houses on the new land created by the filling in of Boston's coves. Into the midst of this boom there came the railroad—suddenly, in the summer of 1835—when Boston's first three lines, to Lowell, Worcester, and Providence, began operating within weeks of one another.

The railroads themselves encouraged a tremendous burst of activity, and new industries clustered around their termini. Where rails from the north penetrated the area of the old millpond, newly named Haymarket Square, machinists and cabinetmakers established shops or relocated from other parts of the city. Railroads from the south and west accelerated the filling of the South Cove between Kneeland Street, where the Worcester and Plymouth roads terminated, and Roxbury. Albany Street, laid out by the South Cove Corporation when Worcester trains reached the New York capital, became the new South Cove waterfront and the location of numerous lumber and coal wharves. Here were built the shops of dozens of carpenters and housewrights who made their fortune constructing housing on the new land of the South End. With them came the factories of the piano industry, the South End's single largest manufacturing business, for which the new and rapidly expanding immigrant population provided a seemingly inexhaustible labor supply.

The railroads also accelerated the flow of goods through Boston, and the heavy demand for raw cotton by the region's inland mills gave the port a marked advantage over other seacoast cities. Southern ports imported increasing quantities of Massachusetts pork and beef, boots and shoes, furniture and wooden ware, almost all of which came through Boston. In addition, such bulk products as ice and granite from Charlestown and Boston wharves made salable ballast for south-bound vessels that might otherwise have chosen other ports. The 1840s saw the climax of both coastwise and foreign commerce. Wharf property was the most productive real estate in Boston, and massive granite warehouses were constructed along the waterfront. In the midst of this "Golden Age of Boston mercantilism," in 1846, the new and beautiful Custom House at the head of Long Wharf opened.

Even while Boston maritime commerce was at its height, however, it was being undercut by rail rates. Increasingly Boston shipping was being diverted to New York, a port closer to much of the nation's interior as well as to southern ports. As coastwise shipping declined, so did the value of wharf property. The clipper-ship era, the most visible result of the discovery of gold in California and Australia, proved the swan song of Boston shipping. The provisioning of California settlers with foodstuffs, clothing, furniture, and other necessities became a substantial business in Boston as elsewhere, and the commerce required the speed for which the clippers were famous.

The annexation of nearby communities, beginning with Roxbury in 1868, forced an extension of Boston's water and sewer facilities. The expanded horsecar services, the growth of the labor force in these outlying areas, and the large plots of available land induced many industries to relocate here or to nearby communities north of the Charles and Mystic rivers. New rail connections and filled land also made Charlestown and East and South Boston attractive ports.

In the last quarter of the 19th century, much of Boston Proper's industrial activity was concentrated in the North and South ends of the city. In the South End, the number of piano factories continued to increase as improvements in the design of the upright brought good instruments within the financial range of middle-class America. In the North End, the growth of the Italian community after 1880 provided a stimulus for the last real period of industrial construction in Boston Proper. Beginning in the 1890s, bakeries (egg macaroni had been introduced in 1881) and confectionery factories were major employers of Italian labor. By 1920 the workplaces of these two industries ringed the North End.

The factors that affected New England manufacturers in general in the early 20th century also struck Boston Proper. The furniture, piano, and shoe industries moved west to be closer to the center of the national market, or south to take advantage of cheaper labor costs. In the 1920s much of Boston Proper's industrial building stock began to be converted to loft space. After 1930, with Boston's economy stagnant and her manufacturing base in decay, very little new private construction took place for nearly thirty years.

Opposite page: A composite map of Boston Proper, showing the shoreline and salt meadows in 1776 together with political boundaries prior to the 1874 annexation of Roxbury. Numbered locations refer to text entries. Adapted from the BOSTON SOUTH Quadrangle of the U.S. Geological Survey and Henry Pelham's *A Plan of Boston in New England with its Environs* (London, 1777).

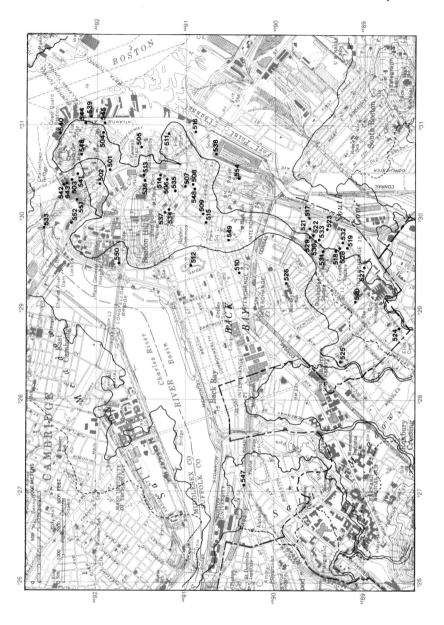

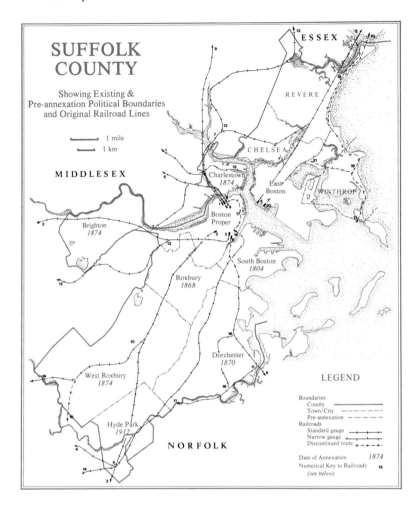

A schematic view of railroads and municipal boundaries. Both have gone through permutations that are not reflected here. Railroad dates reflect the opening of the line; a span of dates indicates that different parts of the line opened at different times. It took several years before either the Fitchburg or the Eastern railroads built stations at the present North Station site on Causeway Street. Although some initial name changes are indicated for clarity's sake, the later absorption of most of the lines into either the Boston & Maine or New York, New Haven & Hartford systems is omitted.

1. Boston & Lowell (1835)
2. Boston & Worcester (1835) (Boston & Albany, 1867)
3. Boston & Providence (1835)
4. Dedham Branch (1834)
5. Eastern (1838) (to Causeway St., 1854)
6. Charlestown Branch (1842) (Fitchburg, 1843; to Causeway St., 1848)
7. Grand Junction (1844–56)
8. Old Colony (1845)
9. Boston & Maine (1845)
10. West Roxbury Branch (1848)
11. Dorchester & Milton Branch (1848)
12. Charles River Branch (1852)
13. Saugus Branch (1853)
14. Midland (1855) (New York & New England, 1873)
15. Mystic River (1870)
16. Shawmut Branch (1872)
17. Union Freight (1872)
18. Eastern Junction, Broad Sound & Point Shirley (1882)
19. Needham Branch (1906)
20. Boston, Revere Beach & Lynn (1872; narrow gauge)
21. Boston, Winthrop & Point Shirley (1877–82; narrow gauge)

501   The Boston Stone

BOSTON SOUTH

9 Marshall Street at Creek Square ^{3}30590.^{46}91760

The earliest surviving evidence of industry along what once was Mill Creek is the Boston Stone, a spherical stone grinder, or "muller," and a stone trough in which the muller ground oil and pigment into paint (figure 1).

Thomas Child, a Roxbury painter, purchased the Marshall Street property in 1692, probably establishing a shop at this location soon afterward. The stones, along with a carved wooden plaque exhibiting the coat of arms of the ancient guild of painters, are thought to have been brought from England about 1701, since the plaque included both Child's initials and the date 1701. Thomas Child died in 1706, but the paint mill became a Boston landmark (literally and figuratively) and a favorite topic of 19th-century Boston guidebooks.

About 1737, Child's estate fell into the hands of a Joseph Howe, who found the stone trough at the bottom of his yard. As a protection against passing vehicles, Howe incorporated the stone into the corner of his house. According to Howe's daughter, still living in 1835, a neighbor who had lived in England and seen the famous London Stone in front of Saint Swithin's Church, which had long been a popular designation for local businesses, proposed that the paint mill be made a similar landmark by adding the inscription "Boston Stone 1737." The stone was so marked and for nearly a century was used for this purpose and occasionally as a starting point for surveyors.

In 1835 the muller, which had been lost for many years, was discovered during excavations for the foundations of the present Marshall Street building, and the two stones together were incorporated into the new building's brick wall. The original stone trough, which was said to have held about two barrels, was broken into four pieces in 1835, and only a small fragment of the original survives. The building itself, 114–120 Blackstone Street, was probably the first building to be constructed after the laying out of Blackstone Street in 1835.

502   Paine Furniture Company

BOSTON SOUTH

48–70 Canal Street ^{3}30350.^{46}91960

About 1805 Mill Creek became the southern end of the Middlesex Canal. Lumber previously portaged down the Merrimack River through Newburyport could now be sent directly to Boston. Among those to benefit were cabinetmakers, who in the decades after 1804 set up shop in the Mill Creek (later Blackstone Street) vicinity. One of the later arrivals on Blackstone Street was Leonard B. Shearer (c. 1808–1864), a cabinetmaker who moved here in 1835. From this event the Paine Furniture Company, the leading furniture manufacturer in Boston in the late 19th century, dates its establishment. John S. Paine (1823–1903) joined Shearer in 1845. A few years later, pressed for space, the firm opened a new shop on Haymarket Square.

Haymarket Square had been laid out in 1839 on filled land at the southern end of the old North Cove millpond. A major attraction to the area was the construction of the Boston & Maine Railroad's brick depot in 1845, and in the late 1840s and 1850s the area attracted a large number of businesses. Shearer and Paine first built on the present Canal Street site, facing the B&M station, about 1854.

After Shearer's death in 1864, Paine conducted the business under his own name, turning increasingly from jobbing to retail sales. Paine spent 1869 in Europe establishing manufacturing connections, and in 1871 he built the existing five-and-a-half-story brick furniture factory and showroom. Measuring 165 × 200 feet in size, the building straddles the block between Canal and Friend streets, with entrances to both streets (figure 2). The building was capped with a mansard roof featuring corner and central pavilions on all four sides. The building's design is attributed to William G. Preston.

The year Paine's new factory opened there were 82 furniture makers in Boston employing 1,498 workers. Ten years later both numbers had increased by over 50%. Despite the firm's increasing emphasis on retail sales, the company continued to manufacture a wide range of household, church, hotel, and office furniture. They specialized, the firm noted in 1893, "in parlor suits in antique and the newest modern designs in elaborately carved work."

The furniture manufacturing industry in Boston entered a slow decline in the 1890s, though Paine's continued to manufacture some product lines into the 1930s. In 1913–14 the firm built a store on the newly fashionable Park Square, where they remain today. The Canal Street store was subdivided for commercial uses, a function it still retains. Much of the Haymarket Square area has since been demolished, but the Paine factory and showrooms, once the center of Boston's 19th-century furniture-making industry, remains as an important landmark.

503   Braman, Dow & Company: Boston Steam & Gas Pipe Works

BOSTON SOUTH

239 Causeway Street ^{3}30360.^{46}92230

The establishment of the Boston & Maine depot at Haymarket Square proved a significant magnet for the introduction of new machine shops in the area, producing a wide variety of machinery and tools. By 1861 there were seven machine shops on Haverhill Street, which ran along the station's east side.

The Boston Steam & Gas Pipe Works was one of the earliest such shops to locate on Haymarket Square and is today the oldest manufacturer of steam pipes and fittings in the country. The works were established in 1848 by two of the leading workmen of Walworth & Nason (**000**), the pioneer pipe and steam heating firm. Founders of the new pipe works were Oliver S. Barrett, a maker of brass pipes, and Jason Braman and John Perham of Cambridgeport. (Nahum M. Dow was clerk, and the company took its present name when Dow was admitted as partner in 1857.) The premises the firm acquired appear to have been those of the second and last Boston foundry of Daniel Badger before he moved to New York about 1848. (See **504**, **506**.)

In 1898 the old B&M station was replaced by the Tremont Subway's northern incline (**534**). The proximity of the pipe works to the station was probably responsible for its two-block move in that year to its present five-story brick block on Causeway Street. The building itself, 85 × 155 feet, had been constructed in 1883 as a rubber-goods warehouse for the Boston Rubber Shoe Company of Malden (**000**). Its architect was the Bostonian Thomas W. Silloway (1828–1910), better known for his ecclesiastical architecture than for his industrial designs. In their new building, Braman, Dow & Company advertised themselves as "manufacturers and dealers in plain and galvanized wrought-iron pipe and fittings and all goods used in connection with steam, gas, or water." A five-alarm fire completely gutted the building in February 1913. The 24-inch-thick firewalls prevented the total loss of the structure, and the building was rebuilt. Charring from the fire is still evident in the attic.

Braman, Dow & Company remains in existence at the same location and is now one of the oldest manufacturing firms in Boston. While its major product line continues to be pipes, valves, and fittings the results of modern materials technology are evident, for these products are now made available in a wide variety of steels and plastics as well as fiberglass and plastic-lined steel. The firm has added a Valve Repair and Automation Division and a full branch warehouse operation in Scarborough, Maine.

504   George T. McLauthlin Company, machinists and elevator manufacturers (cast-iron facade)

120 Fulton Street

BOSTON SOUTH

^{3}30920.^{46}91920

The McLauthlin Elevator building is probably the earliest and is certainly the finest surviving example of cast-iron architecture in Boston. Daniel Badger was the first in Boston to use cast iron in the construction of a storefront, in 1842 (see **506**), and by the 1850s its use here seems to have become fairly widespread. The earliest architectural uses imitated stone construction, often copying in spirit if not in fact the buildings of the Italian Renaissance. Like New York City's more celebrated Haughwout Building (1856, Architectural Iron Works, foundry), the five-story iron facade features a repeating round-arch window bay on the second, third, and fourth floors reminiscent of a Venetian palazzo. This construction not only provided large window areas, but also lent itself readily to inexpensive multiple castings. Today there are six known examples of cast-iron architecture in Boston.

Neither the architect nor the foundry that cast the facade are known. Traditionally, the McLauthlin building has been dated 1861, the year in which George T. McLauthlin moved to Fulton Street. The year 1856, when William Adams & Company moved to 120 Fulton Street from a location about a block distant, has also been suggested. William Adams & Company were an established firm of machinists whose earlier location at the corner of Cross and Fulton streets was adjacent to Daniel Badger's 1830 foundry.

George T. McLauthlin (1826–1895) was born in Duxbury but spent most of his childhood in East Bridgewater. The grandson of Jesse Reed, an inventor of nail and tack machines, McLauthlin developed an early aptitude for building shoe machinery and then water wheels. In 1852 he established an office in Boston, moving his works to East Boston in 1858. The works were destroyed by fire in 1861, and McLauthlin immediately purchased the works and business of William Adams & Company, in so doing adding the manufacture of steam engines and elevators to his earlier line of water wheels and other machinery.

The business was greatly expanded in 1878 when McLauthlin purchased the business of the J. C. Hoadley Company, a Lawrence manufacturer of the portable steam engines invented by John Chipman Hoadley (1818–1886). Hoadley remained as consulting engineer to McLauthlin until his death.

The manufacture of elevators had been introduced in 1861. By the early 20th century, under the founder's nephew, Martin B. McLauthlin, the design, manufacture, and installation of freight and passenger elevators became the firm's chief business. Among the firm's installations was the stage mechanism of the Boston Opera House (1909), including stage and orchestra lifts, a stage-setting mechanism, aerial bridges, and panorama operating devices. The company remained in Boston until 1977, when it moved its operations to Cambridge, where they remain today. In 1978–79 the building was converted to 20 condominiums, one of the earliest historic rehabilitations in Boston certified by the National Park Service.

505   Richards Building (cast-iron facade)

BOSTON SOUTH

114 State Street ^{3}30770.^{46}91480

Like the McLauthlin Building, the Richards Building features a cast-iron facade in the North Italian mode of the Renaissance Revival style, with a repeated arched window-bay motif, each bay being supported by fluted engaged columns (figure 3). Originally five stories high with a mansard roof, the building had two additional stories added in 1889.

Lower State Street, at the head of Long Wharf and (since 1846) the site of the Custom House, has been the center of commercial trading in Boston since the 18th century. For much of the early 19th century, the property at 114 State Street was owned by Robert Gould Shaw, father of the Civil War officer of the same name who died leading a regiment of black soldiers at the siege of Fort Wagner in 1863. Shaw was a commission merchant on the waterfront and head of the firm of R. G. Shaw & Company. After his death in 1853, the property passed to his daughter and son-in-law. The building was probably constructed about 1859, for it was in that year that Gardiner H. Shaw and Quincy A. Shaw, two members of R. G. Shaw & Co., were listed at 114 State Street. Beginning in that year, a succession of manufacturing and commercial firms were also listed as having offices in the building. In 1870 East Boston's Atlantic Works (**000**) had an office here. The building took its present name in 1889 when it was purchased by Calvin A. Richards (1828–1892), former president of the Metropolitan Street Railway. After the absorption of most of Boston's streetcar lines into the West End Street Railway in 1889, Richards retired to private life, purchasing and remodeling the building that now bears his name. Completed in January 1890, the chief alteration was the two-story addition. The new sheet-metal facade, flanked by two-story oriel windows, was supplied by E. B. Badger & Sons. (Erastus Badger was a distant cousin of Daniel Badger [**506**].) The original first-floor storefront, covered over since 1919, was restored to view in 1983.

506   Boston Post Building (cast-iron facade)

BOSTON SOUTH
17 Milk Street ^{3}30410.^{46}91220

Completed in 1874, the Boston Post Building is the only one of Boston's six surviving cast-iron facades for which the foundry is known. Architect of the Victorian Gothic building was the noted Boston firm of Peabody & Stearns. The foundry, still identified by its name plate, was New York City's celebrated Architectural Iron Works, founded by Daniel D. Badger (1806–1884). Badger was a pioneer in the use of cast iron for building purposes and was no stranger to Boston, where he introduced it. Born in Portsmouth, New Hampshire, Badger established a shop in Boston, at the corner of Fulton and Cross streets, about 1830. Here he advertised "the manufacture of wrought iron in all its branches." In this business he was very successful, and he soon turned to the use of cast iron as a building material. In 1842 Badger constructed the first cast-iron storefront in Boston for a building on Washington Street. About 1846 he moved to New York, where he continued to manufacture architectural cast iron on a large scale.

The Great Fire that swept through 65 acres of downtown Boston in November 1872 found its northern boundary at Milk Street, where a heroic and eventually successful effort was made to save the Old South Meeting House from the flames. Not so favored was the *Boston Post*, whose newspaper offices stood not far distant, at the corner of Devonshire and Water streets. Founded in 1831 by Colonel Charles Green, the *Post* was Boston's leading Democratic newspaper by the 1870s. After the fire the *Post* moved to Milk Street, constructing there the existing five-story building, later altered with the addition of a sixth story (figure 4).

The site the paper chose to build upon had been known as the birthplace of Benjamin Franklin in 1706. The newspaper chose to memorialize the event, and the elaborate Gothic-style facade prominently features a bust of Franklin between the second and third stories. The second and third stories also feature an abundance of Neo-Grec and Eastlake-inspired ornament, though the upper floors have seen a succession of later alterations. The *Post* installed its presses in the basement, establishing editorial rooms on the fourth floor and composition on the fifth. The second and third floors were occupied by other firms and offices.

The building was used by the *Post* until 1905, when the newspaper moved to larger quarters. No. 17 then was acquired by the *Boston Evening Transcript*, located next door at the corner of Washington Street. The *Transcript* occupied the building until its bankruptcy in 1941. In 1982 the building underwent rehabilitation as professional offices under the preservation incentives of the Economic Recovery Act of 1981.

507   40–46 Summer Street (cast-iron facade)

BOSTON SOUTH
$^330370.^{46}90920$

Buildings along virtually the entire length of Summer Street were consumed in the 1872 fire. Among the first to be erected in the following year was this five-story High Victorian cast-iron commercial building. Above the first floor, the facade remains largely as built, including the cast date 1873. The architect was Charles K. Kirby, one of a handful of prominent Boston architects responsible for the rebuilding of the district after the fire. The building's first occupants were members of the dry goods and clothing trade, which dominated the district both before and after 1872.

508   71–73 Summer Street (cast-iron facade)

BOSTON SOUTH
$^330360.^{46}90980$

Another Summer Street cast-iron facade was created for this six-story commercial building, probably also erected in 1873. Typical of the period is the heavily articulated four-bay facade. The third and fourth stories feature fluted half columns on either side of windows with flat tops and rounded corners, set within deep reveals.

George W. Pope is credited as the structure's builder/architect. Born in Kennebunkport, Maine, in 1821, Pope played a prominent role in the development of the South End, building a large number of houses along Tremont Street and Columbus Avenue. After the 1872 fire, he is said to have erected 50 buildings "in a very short time." Owner of the property, both before and after the fire, was Jacob Sleeper (1802–1889), a philanthropist and one of the founders of Boston University in 1869. Sleeper's fortune had come from real-estate transactions and from his business furnishing supplies for the U.S. Navy. Between 1860 and 1883 he was president of the Boston Wharf Co. (**000**). Sleeper left the building to Boston University, which continued for at least 25 years to lease space to the dry-goods trade. The two lower stories were sharply altered in 1952 with the installation of the present glass and granite bank facade.

509   611 Washington Street (cast-iron facade)

BOSTON SOUTH

^{3}30060.^{46}90790

The most heavily altered of Boston's six remaining cast-iron facades is this six-story commercial building constructed between 1874 and 1883. Only the second and third stories retain original architectural detail. The three upper stories appear to have been stripped of surface ornament, leaving planar surfaces. The building, 86 feet in height, features a rounded corner bay where the Washington Street and Fayette Court facades intersect. Though outside the district destroyed by the 1872 fire, the property, owned by a James Parker, remained unbuilt upon until sometime after the publication of the 1874 *Atlas of Suffolk County*.

510   Carter, Dinsmore & Company, ink manufacturers

BOSTON SOUTH

162–172 Columbus Avenue ^{3}29410.^{46}90410

Carter, Dinsmore & Company, more recently known as Carter's Ink Company, was established in 1858 by William Carter, a wholesale paper dealer who that year began to manufacture inks as a sideline. He introduced a popular combined writing and copying fluid, to which he gave the name "Carter's Combined." After service in the Civil War, his nephew John W. Carter (1843–1895) joined the firm. Following the destruction of the plant in 1872, John W. Carter and James P. Dinsmore formed the partnership of Carter, Dinsmore & Company to carry on the ink and adhesive part of William Carter's business. In 1884 they erected the existing plant on Columbus Avenue, adjacent to the site of the Armory of the First Corps of Cadets, built a decade later.

The new ink factory was the work of architect Theodore Minot Clark (1845–1909). Though a native of Boston, Clark had worked in H. H. Richardson's New York office before setting up his own firm in Boston in 1872. Several years later Clark collaborated with Richardson on the design of Trinity Church (1876), and he is said to have been responsible for the church's porch facing Copley Square. Thus it is not surprising that the ink factory on Columbus Avenue shows a strong Richardsonian influence. Five stories high, the brick facade is richly decorated with brownstone and terra-cotta Romanesque ornament. Three round-arch window bays, four stories in height, dominate the Columbus Avenue elevation.

A contemporary directory described the factory as "the largest and best equipped writing ink factory in the world." The basement, in addition to containing boiler and engine rooms, was used for the storage of glass and earthenware and was said to be capable of holding up to five million bottles. The company's offices were on the second floor, while bottling was done on the third. The fifth and sixth stories were utilized as laboratories and tank floors. By 1885 the company had an annual output of over six million bottles of ink and mucilage.

After John Carter's death in 1895, the company was renamed Carter's Ink Company, and about 1910 the company moved to larger quarters in Cambridge (**000**). The "Carter Building" became home for a succession of offices and retail stores. About 1980 the building was rehabilitated for use as the Back Bay Raquette Club.

511   Chadwick Lead Works

BOSTON SOUTH

176–184 High Street ^{3}30890.^{46}91180

In the 1820s the hardware business had been largely confined to the Dock Square area, near Faneuil Hall. After the 1872 fire the tendency of the trade was to locate in the Fort Hill district, and a number of buildings representative of the trade still survive in the High Street area. One of the most architecturally noteworthy examples is the Chadwick Lead Works, constructed in 1887 to the designs of one of Boston's leading architects, William G. Preston (1844–1910). Six stories high and approximately 75 feet square, the brick, stone, and terra-cotta structure is dominated by four five-story arched window bays, features and materials also used three years earlier in the Carter, Dinsmore ink factory. At the rear of the lead works an ornamental shot tower rises another 35 feet above the roof. The words "Chadwick Lead Works" appear prominently in terra cotta on both the main building and the shot tower (figure 5).

Joseph H. Chadwick was born in Roxbury in 1827. In his youth he had been employed by the Boston Lead Company, whose Roxbury works were founded in 1829. In 1862 Chadwick formed Joseph H. Chadwick & Company, reorganized in 1878 as the Chadwick Lead Works. In the latter year the firm moved to Fort Hill Square, locating at 173–175 High Street, on the opposite side of the square from the existing buildings. The chief products of the company, according to an advertisement in 1885, were its "famous 'diamond-brand' white lead, lead pipe, tin pipe, sheet lead, ribbon and tape lead, copper and iron pumps, hydraulic rams, solder, etc." Thirty-five hands were then employed.

The success of the business must have been substantial, for in 1887 the firm built the existing factory on the opposite side of Fort Hill Square. The works included a shot tower for the manufacture of gunshot. A small furnace was located at the top of the tower, behind the terra-cotta plaque identifying the firm.

It is unclear how long manufacturing was actually carried on here. About 1890 the company purchased the Forest River Lead Works in Salem, and after that date factory operations were probably carried on there, though an office was maintained on High Street. In 1901 the company merged with the Boston Lead Company, forming the Chadwick-Boston Lead Company. Offices were moved to Boston Lead's old quarters at the corner of Congress and Franklin streets. Boston Lead's works, at Sheridan Square, Roxbury, remained in use through the 1960s, operated successively by Chadwick-Boston, National-Boston Lead Co., and National Lead Co. of Massachusetts.

The High Street building, after passing through a succession of office and warehouse uses, was historically rehabilitated in 1981 under National Park Service guidelines. Today it and the adjoining warehouse at 172 High Street (built 1875) house professional offices and a successful first-floor restaurant.

512 Public Garden Footbridge

Public Garden, between Charles Street	BOSTON SOUTH
and Commonwealth Avenue	^{3}29470.^{46}90940

One of architect William Preston's earliest designs, in which he collaborated with the young civil engineer Clemens Hershell (1842–1930, and later a nationally known hydraulic engineer), was for the suspension footbridge in the Public Garden, which opened June 1, 1867 (figure 6).

In the original plan the Public Garden, it was intended that there should be a bridge over the pond, continuing and connecting the path from Commonwealth Avenue to Charles Street. In the spring of 1866 a special committee of the Boston City Council sponsored a design competition for such a bridge. Some fifteen designs were submitted, and as the original advertisements did not call for any specific type of design, there was probably considerable variation in the plans. "To come to a decision," the city auditor wrote, "the Commitee decided that the bridge should be high enough to allow skaters to pass under, that the paths along the edges of the pond should not be closed up, that the bridge should be of iron and stone, and finally cost as little as possible." The design chosen was a suspension bridge, 100 feet long and 15 feet wide. Although a single span "would have made a lighter looking and a handsomer bridge," the auditor wrote, it would have cost more than the city was willing to spend. As a result, the bridge was designed with two granite piers supporting a central span, connected to shore anchorages with shorter-half spans. The chains supporting the deck are made up of eye-bars, despite the fact that the use of continuous wire cables in suspension bridges was already two decades old by the time the footbridge was built.

In the early 20th century the deck of the bridge was reinforced with a steel and concrete beam. Thus, while the eye-bar chains have been retained, the structure no longer functions as a suspension bridge. In 1936 the Boston Society of Civil Engineers placed on bronze tablet on the bridge honoring the designers.

513   Ames Building

One Court Street

BOSTON SOUTH
^{3}30470.^{46}91460

The 13-story granite and brick Ames Building, Boston's first skyscraper, represented one solution to the increasing demand for office space in the last decades of the 19th century. To serve the upper floors of the 196-foot building, then the highest ever erected in the city, architects Shepley, Rutan & Coolidge drew on the most recent development in elevator technology: the hydraulic-plunger elevator. The plunger cylinder extended 126 feet down into the bedrock of the Shawmut Peninsula.

The building was named after its developer, Frederick L. Ames of Easton (1835–1893), grandson of the founder of the celebrated Easton shovel works (1803). Ames was better known for his service as director or officer of numerous railroads. The Ames family had been one of architect H. H. Richardson's chief patrons, and Ames employed Richardson's successors, Shepley, Rutan & Coolidge, to design the new office building, which was completed in 1891.

Boston's first skyscraper was conservative by contemporary standards. Unlike skyscrapers then being constructed in New York and Chicago, it was not steel-framed. The street walls were of stone with brick backing, and the three-story base, built of huge granite blocks quarried in Milford, carried a ten-story superstructure faced with Ohio sandstone on the Washington and Court street facades. Inside, the walls of the first floor were of marble, as was the monumental stairway. These stairs led up to a two-story banking room, the most important room in the building, now subdivided into two working floors. The motifs of the Byzantine-Romanesque carvings on the exterior are repeated inside in mosaic work. Little remains of the original interior spaces or decoration, and the early hydraulic elevator has also been replaced.

514   Winthrop Building

BOSTON SOUTH

7 Water Street

^{3}30500.^{46}91290

Boston's first steel-framed building was completed in 1894, a block to the north of the Ames Building.

The nine-story Winthrop Building was designed by Clarence H. Blackall (1857–1942), and its steel-frame construction was determined in part by the extremely narrow lot on which it was built. On Washington Street, the building is 30 feet wide; its opposite end on Devonshire Street is only 20 feet wide. A skeletal steel structure offered a considerable increase in floor area over a building supported by conventional masonry bearing walls.

Blackall adopted the "Z-bar steel column," then the most commonly used form in Chicago, and the immediate predecessor of the rolled H-column, which appeared about 1900. The Z-bar column was made up of four Z-bars riveted to a central web plate. The resulting cross section was essentially an H with half serifs projecting at right angles from each arm. Another unusual feature of the building was the extensive use of wind-bracing. Perhaps because of the narrow width of the building, horizontal steel trusses were built into each floor, and vertical trusses were built into many of the interior partitions.

Except for the Neoclassical limestone entrance, the original first-floor facades were dominated by large areas of glass, and today, on the Devonshire Street end of the building, where a single office takes up the entire first-floor width, this steel and glass construction is plainly visible. The remaining eight stories are sheathed in a masonry skin made of what a contemporary journal called a "pale golden buff brick and fire-flashed terra cotta about the color of a slightly browned bread crust."

The building was given its present name about 1898 to honor the location of Governor John Winthrop's last dwelling (1644) on the adjacent property to the south (now the site of the Old South office building). On Spring Lane, today a pedestrian alley along the rear of the building, was the "Great Spring" that had attracted Winthrop's colony to the Shawmut Peninsula.

515   Edison Electric Illuminating Company: Head Place Station and Office

25–39 Boylston Street	BOSTON SOUTH ^{3}29970.^{46}90750

Head Place is a small alley off Boylston Street in Boston's theater district. It was here that the Edison Electric Illuminating Company of Boston (now the Boston Edison Company) established its first generating station in February 1886.

Organized two months before, the company moved into an existing two-story structure on Head Place. The plant's original equipment consisted of a 90-hp Armington & Sims engine driving two Edison "type H" dynamos, which together produced about 76 kilowatts. Head Place seems to have been chosen for its location in the theater district, naturally a prime market for electric light. The company's first customer was the nearby Bijou Theatre, for which Thomas Edison had built an "isolated" generating plant four years before, making it the first theater in America to be lit throughout by electricity.

In the early 1880s electric lighting was in its infancy. The earliest generating stations were "isolated" plants designed for single customers, such as the Bijou. Edison first proposed a central power station in 1878, but it was not until 1882 that he started building such stations. The first was New York City's Pearl Street Station. By 1886, four smaller cities in Massachusetts had central stations, but the large cities were less eager to commit the necessary capital. Boston, already served by several small companies, was only the second large city to be tackled by Edison interests, and much of the capital for the new company came from New York.

Thomas Edison made frequent inspection trips to Boston in the early years of the company. In 1887 he appointed Charles Leavitt Edgar (1860–1932) as general manager. Edgar served in that capacity and later as president of the company for nearly fifty years, and the company's expansion in that period was due in large measure to his executive and engineering genius. Under his guidance, the company pioneered in many generating developments that became standard central-station practice, and Edgar himself became known as one of the most progressive central-station managers in this country or abroad. (See **516, 546**.)

The Head Place Station was enlarged in 1887 and again in 1890, but after the completion of the new turbine plant at L Street (**000**), the station was relegated in 1905 to the status of a district substation. As the use of DC power declined, the need for separate substations vanished, and the Head Place facility was torn down about 1947. Remaining at the site is the company's first office, built in 1907 to the designs of the Boston firm of Winslow & Bigelow, the partnership that handled all the Edison Electric Illuminating Company construction. In 1923, the 10-story building was enlarged to the east by the firm's successor, Bigelow & Wadsworth. The structure remained in use as Boston Edison offices through the 1950s, when it was sold and converted to stores and offices.

516   Edison Electric Illuminating Company: Atlantic Avenue Station

BOSTON SOUTH

500 Atlantic Avenue ^{3}30950.^{46}90850

A year after the opening of the Head Place Station, the Edison Company opened a second generating plant on Hawkins Street (now replaced) to serve the northern part of the city. Almost a duplicate of the first station, the new plant furnished 1440 kilowatts to the business district north of State Street, the limit of the Head Place station's territory. In the spring of 1890, company manager Charles Edgar spent several months visiting European generating plants. The outcome of this investigation was the company's third station, located between Atlantic Avenue and Fort Point Channel. It was begun in 1891 and represented the first real advance in station capacity and design.

Completed in August 1892, this third station was equipped with four triple-expansion vertical condensing engines, to which were coupled eight direct-drive generators with a combined capacity of 1600 kw. This station was looked upon as a great departure in the electric lighting industry, since these slow-speed vertical engines were the first ones built on this side of the Atlantic, and the direct-connected units were among the first in the history of the business. The size of the engine room, its ideal location on the waterfront, and its modern facilities for handling and storing coal created widespread interest among engineers throughout the country.

Edgar went to Europe again in 1893 to investigate the use of storage batteries as auxiliaries to large central stations. So impressed was he with their performance that he had one installed in the Atlantic Avenue station in 1894, the first of its kind in the country. A second was installed at Head Place in 1895. These batteries proved so useful at stations then existing that it was decided to provide battery substations in the outlying districts in order to increase the capacity of the system. The first battery plant was the fourth district station, located on Scotia Street in the Back Bay (now demolished), opened in August 1896. Storage batteries allowed the system to be expanded to include territory that would have been inaccessible to a company still using exclusively direct current.

The virtues of direct and alternating current were vigorously debated in the late 1880s and the 1890s. In 1886 Westinghouse had established the first AC generating stations in the country in Great Barrington, Massachusetts, and Greensburg, Pennsylvania; and two years later the Edison Company's chief rival in Boston, the Boston Electric Light Company, had inaugurated AC service. Not until 1899, however, after its rival had built its L Street (AC) generating plant (**000**), did the company feel sufficiently threatened to propose installing some AC capacity in its expansion of the Atlantic Avenue plant. The acquisition of the L Street property by the company in 1902 eliminated this need.

The capacity of the Atlantic Avenue station was increased to 10,400 kw in 1900–1901. In 1905 both the Head Place and Hawkins Street generating stations were converted to district substations supplied with DC current from Atlantic Avenue, which now supplied a territory within a radius of 4000 feet. All other territory was supplied with AC from L Street.

The use of DC power in downtown Boston reached its peak in the late 1930s. With the conversion of many installations to AC operation, demand for DC declined. DC generation was discontinued altogether about 1973. Today the remaining DC load is served by AC-fed rectifiers located in vaults beneath the streets. The Atlantic Avenue station was demolished in the early 1970s. Since then the site has been used as one of the company's five "network" transformer stations, converting 115 kv to the 14 kv volts of the feeder network.

517   Joseph F. Paul & Company: Bay State Moulding Mills

BOSTON SOUTH

365 Albany Street ^{3}30000.^{46}89600

The South End, the largest extant Victorian urban neighborhood in the country, was the first major residential district in Boston Proper to be developed on filled land. Although the "necklands" on either side of Washington Street had been laid out in streets as early as 1814, the region developed slowly until about 1850, when the city began to auction off the land to real estate developers.

All this construction activity attracted numerous carpenters and housewrights. Among the earliest was Joseph F. Paul (1823–1889). A native of Kittery, Maine, Paul came to Boston at an early age. By 1847 he was established as a housewright at the corner of Tremont and Appleton streets, close to Bay Village, whose Paul Street (now Paul Place) was probably named after the builder. By 1851 he had formed a partnership with John J. McNutt. Paul & McNutt were among the pioneers in the business of mill planing and working lumber by machinery for building and other purposes. The partnership was dissolved in 1858, and McNutt left to form the Novelty Wood Works (**518**). Paul then organized the Bay State Moulding Mills, a business that became, his obituary claimed, "one of the largest manufacturing establishments in this line in New England." In 1872 he moved the business to Albany Street, then a waterfront location on South Bay. On the east side of Albany Street he built the Bay State Wharf for lumber and coal schooners. Opposite the wharf, at the corner of Bristol Street, he built an ornate Second Empire-style four-story brick mill with corner towers, designed by William G. Preston. From the start Paul seems to have planned to lease out space. The Bay State Organ Company, organized in 1872 by veterens of the Smith American Organ Company (**526**), was here for sixteen years. From 1888 to 1906, Cole & Woodberry (formerly of the Hook & Hastings Organ Co.), and then James Cole, produced a well-known series of church organs here.

The existing four-story brick factory was completed in 1911 on the foundations of the earlier building. Architect for the mill was Samuel D. Kelley, who has also produced the plans for the Everett Piano Company's factory (**532**) nearby. The firm of Joseph F. Paul & Company operated a planing mill here until about 1930. For a number of years the building housed a designer of window displays, and it is today operated by a paint distributor.

518   Novelty Wood Works

BOSTON SOUTH

38 Wareham Street ^{3}29640.^{46}89300

Joseph Paul's earliest partner, John J. McNutt (1822–1894), was born in Truro, Nova Scotia. At the age of 20 he came to Boston, where two years later he joined Paul on Tremont Street. After the partnership was dissolved, McNutt formed the Novelty Wood Works, building a new plant on Wareham Street. The location, on the South Bay waterfront, was rapidly becoming the center of the woodworking industry in Boston.

The McNutt Building, constructed in 1863, was the first brick building erected for woodworking purposes in the South End. Designed and built by McNutt, who often acted as architect as well as builder, the building is a minor architectural landmark of the district. In addition to conventional buildings and interiors, the firm did all kinds of theatrical woodwork, and the building's design shows something of this interest. The building is three stories in height, and the principal Harrison Street facade originally featured a central cupola above the existing pair of round-arch brownstone windows. Still extant is the wooden second-floor balcony, with shaped balusters, running nearly the length of the building. The balcony is approached by an exterior stair on one end, originally curved. The Wareham Street facade features cast-iron beam anchors in the form of heraldic shields, each with the bas-relief image of a raised arm clutching a hammer—the heraldic device of the Massachusetts Charitable Mechanic Association, founded in 1795.

For his generosity to brother builders and carpenters in financial difficulties, McNutt won the soubriquet "the father of Wareham Street." By the early 1890s McNutt employed more than 200 workmen, conducting every branch of the woodworking industry. The firm built numerous buildings including hotels, theaters, and the Cyclorama (**526**), as well as many large manufacturing plants in Chelsea, Revere, Roxbury, South Boston, and Neponset.

After McNutt's death in 1894, the business was carried on for a few years by his son, though in smaller quarters on the opposite side of Wareham Street. Since 1924 the McNutt Building has housed the Charak Furniture Company, incorporated in 1920 by Estey P. and Jacob Charak.

519   William F. Badger Planing Works

BOSTON SOUTH

531–541 Albany Street   ³29680.⁴⁶89180

William F. Badger (1833–1897) was born in Chelsea, Vermont. He came to Boston in the early 1850s, taking up the business of building stairs. In 1856 he went into business for himself on Tremont Street, near Dover Street. His first job was to make and set up stairs for the houses of the Twenty Associates, the founders of Hyde Park, and Badger built himself a house in Hyde Park the same year. Outgrowing his shop on Tremont Street, he built a larger one on Wareham Street about 1864, and he remained there for thirty years, eventually expanding the stair-building business to include a wide variety of "builders' finish"—the moldings, windows, doors and door frames, paneling and washstands, stairs, rails, and balusters that could be turned out with planing and turning equipment. In this line Badger was reputed to be the oldest manufacturer in Boston.

Having acquired the property at the corner of Albany and Wareham streets, Badger constructed the existing five-story brick planing mill in 1888. It was while constructing an addition to this plant, in August 1897, that he fell 20 feet from a staging; he died shortly thereafter.

For a few years the building continued to be operated as a woodworking shop, but by the late 1920s the Estabrook Building, as it became known, had been subdivided for a variety of smaller firms, a use that continues today.

520   Pray Brothers Carriage Factory/Central Storage Warehouse

BOSTON SOUTH

32–36 East Concord Street at James Street   ³29080.⁴⁶89090

Joseph F. Pray (1832–1904) was one of about 48 carriage builders in Boston in 1870. His father, Joseph C. Pray, had entered the business in 1845, and in 1863 his son succeeded him. In 1872 Boston's leading carriage builder, Thomas Goddard, retired, and Pray purchased the business, keeping on Goddard's workmen. To accommodate the expanded business Pray built a new brick carriage factory at the corner of East Concord and James streets with the financial assistance of his brother. Pray's move into the heart of the South End must have been motivated in part by the expectation that a wealthy clientele would be moving there. His mansard-roofed two-story factory copies in a minor way the splendor of the French Second Empire-style hotel, the

St. James, built four years earlier at the other end of the James Street block. But the popularity of the South End was rapidly being eclipsed by that of the new Back Bay, to which Pray moved in 1878. The St. James itself had closed by 1882, when it was purchased by the New England Conservatory of Music.

Pray's successor on East Concord Street was J. Theodore Gurney, a Roxbury carriage maker with a reputation in the trade as "a great talker" and of little financial standing. However, Gurney won a substantial contract to build carriages for the Herdic Phaeton Company, and he probably used that opportunity to move into Pray's old quarters. A year later he was reported doing considerable business for the cab companies, who advanced him money to buy stock. By 1886 the property was heavily mortgaged, and within six years it was again vacant. In 1892 the building was converted to commercial storage as the Central Storage Warehouse, a use it retained until the 1970s. The building is now vacant.

521   Reed's Block

BOSTON SOUTH
2–66 Thayer Street ^{3}29920.^{46}89620

Reed's Block is probably the earliest example in Boston of a building designed specifically to house a variety of small industrial firms. Built in 1880–81, the building is 634 feet in length, stretching the entire block between Harrison Avenue and Albany Street. It was, its developer boasted, "the longest building in the city" and "the only complete building yet erected in Boston expressly for manufacturing." Four stories in height and 50 feet in width, the brick and granite building was divided into nine separate sections, with section one at Albany Street and section nine at Harrison Avenue. The middle (fifth) section housed the boiler and engine room, which supplied steam and motive power to the manufacturers in the building. Several of the original tenants later expanded into larger quarters. One of the most important of these was John Reece, whose buttonhole machinery company (see **522**) was housed on three floors of section nine. Thirty-nine other firms also had shops in the building in 1885.

The building was named in honor of Gideon F. T. Reed (1817–1892), one of the original owners. Reed had been the Paris partner of what then was Tiffany, Reed & Co., the New York jewelry firm. In 1878 he retired to a house in Jamaica Plain, Massachusetts. Although it was Reed's name that was displayed in granite letters on the Harrison

Avenue facade, Eliot B. Mayo (1848–1896) was the building's chief developer, and the initials E.B.M. and the date 1880 figure prominently in the center of the long Thayer Street facade. In addition to maintaining an office on Doane Street, Mayo also had an office in the building's section six near the middle of the block.

The building continues to be used by small manufacturers to this day.

522   Reece Buttonhole Machine Company

BOSTON SOUTH

500–502 Harrison Avenue ^{3}29770.^{46}89580

The Canadian John C. Reece (1853–1896) came to the United States at an early age. Between 1877 and 1880 he devised a radical improvement in existing buttonhole machines, an important part of the women's garment and shoe industries. Reece replaced the loop stitch by the lock stitch and caused the needle to travel around the buttonhole (instead of the buttonhole revolving around the needle, as had been the case previously). A company was formed in 1881, and in the 1880s and 1890s Reece machines won numerous awards. By 1893 the company's works in the Reed Block were said to be one of the largest establishments of their kind in the world.

The present five-story brick factory, 70 × 350 feet, was begun in November 1895 and completed the following spring. The structure's building permit lists the contractor Frederick N. Footman as architect and Whidden & Co. of 101 Milk Street as builder. Tragically, the company's founder fell to his death in an elevator shaft in the new building less than a week before it was to open. Reece's name, following the style of Reed's Block, is memorialized in granite letters on both the Harrison Avenue and Randolph Street facades.

After Reece's death, the company continued to make improvements in buttonhole machinery. By 1930 Reece machines, some capable of 300 shapes and sizes of buttonholes, enabled a single operator to make 8,000 holes a day. That year close to 500 people were employed. About 1949 the company built a new factory in Waltham, to which it moved its offices in the mid-1950s. Until it left the area in 1982, the Reece Corporation was a leading manufacturer of buttonhole, pocket welting, and specialized sewing equipment, with an employee roster numbering 1,100 men and women. Since the 1950s the Harrison Avenue building has housed a succession of light industrial firms.

523   Goodyear Shoe Machinery Company

BOSTON SOUTH

443 Albany Street ^{3}29870.^{46}89400

A year after Reece completed his buttonhole machine plant, the Goodyear Shoe Machinery Company built a four-story brick factory about
a block distant, to manufacture the Goodyear welting machines. The
company had been organized by Charles Goodyear (1833–1896), eldest
son of the inventor of vulcanization (see **000**). Goodyear had experi-
mented with adapting the sewing machine for sewing welts, the leather
strip inserted between the outer and inner soles and the upper. The
first practical machine of this type was developed by Christian Dancel
in 1874. "Machine welted shoes," the company advertised in 1890,
"possess all the advantages of hand-sewed, having no nails, pegs, wax
thread, or tacks inside to hurt the feet or wear out the stockings."

The new plant, 65 × 345 feet and 64 feet high, opened in the spring
of 1897, though the company remained an independent entity for
only two more years. By 1899 the making of shoe machinery was
controlled by three large companies: the Goodyear Shoe Machinery
Company, the Consolidated & McKay Lasting Machine Company, and
the McKay Shoe Machinery Company. Each made and leased machines
adapted to a particular group of operations. In 1900 these firms joined
forces as the United Shoe Machinery Company, which for over half
a century dominated the machine business of the shoe and leather
industry. The new firm constructed a large plant in Beverly in 1905
but retained the Harrison Avenue factory until after World War I.

524   Green Shoe Manufacturing Company

BOSTON SOUTH

960 Harrison Avenue ^{3}28790.^{46}88600

In the last half of the 19th century, the development of shoemaking
machinery led to important changes in the organization of the shoe
industry. Increasingly, as the decades progressed, the shoemaking
process was transformed into a series of small tasks performed by
machines operated by semiskilled or unskilled workers. Shoemaking
machinery freed the industry from the traditional centers of skilled
labor, such as Lynn and Brockton. By the turn of the century Boston,
too, had become an important shoemaking center. Between 1899 and
1909 the value of shoes produced in Boston more than tripled. By
1914 Boston ranked fourth in the nation (after Brockton, Lynn, and
New York City) in the value of shoes produced. Although Boston's

rank in relation to other cities declined after that, the industry continued to expand until 1928. In 1924 shoe factories employed more workers than any other industry in Boston.

It was in 1924 that the Green Shoe Manufacturing Company erected the exisiting five-story brick and steel-frame shoe factory on Harrison Avenue, close to the old Roxbury line. The company had been founded five years before by Jacob Slosberg and Philip Green and had erected its first plant in Roxbury. There the firm employed 150–200 workers and had a capacity of 2,000 pairs of shoes per day. The move to Harrison Avenue in 1924 doubled that output. The company specialized in women's and children's shoes. In the 1950s the company expanded to the north, building a five-story addition larger than the entire plant built to that date. Renamed the Stride Rite Corporation in 1972, the company is still one of the largest shoe manufacturers in the country, with 6,000 employees nationwide. Today the company's largest manufacturing facilities are in Maine and Missouri, though plants also are operated in Lawrence and Brockton.

525   Chickering & Sons Piano Factory

791 Tremont Street

BOSTON SOUTH
^{3}28440.^{46}89260

The most famous of Boston's many piano manufacturers was Jonas Chickering (1797–1853), often credited as the founder of the piano industry in the United States. His fame rests largely on a group of key inventions patented in the last decade of his life, including the one-piece cast-iron frame for grand pianos in 1843 and overstringing (by which the bass division of the strings is made to cross over the tenor part in order to allow them a greater length in a limited space) in 1850.

Trained as a cabinetmaker in his native New Hampshire, Chickering came to Boston in 1818. For three years he studied pianomaking with John Osborn, the pioneer Boston piano manufacturer who had learned the business in turn from Benjamin Crehore of Milton. In 1823 Chickering set up in business for himself on Tremont Street, next to the King's Chapel Burying Ground. By the 1840s he employed over 100 people and had become known as the most experienced piano manufacturer in the United States. The Chickering factory was destroyed by fire in December 1852. Chickering himself died in December of the following year before the new factory could be completed, and the business was carried on by his sons, Thomas E., Charles F., and George H. Chickering.

Completed in 1854 to the designs of Holliston-born architect Edwin Payson (1818–1867), the new brick piano factory was said to be the largest building in North America, but for the U.S. Capitol. Built around a large open courtyard, the building measures 250 feet on a side. Each of the three principal elevations is five stories in height, and the Tremont Street facade features an elaborate Italianate cupola above the central entrance. The two-story fourth side contained the plant's boiler and engine rooms. The building opened with an initial staff of 400 workers. On the top floor, where there was a minimum of dust and disturbance, was the varnishing area, where piano cases were finished prior to their descent to floors below. In this process, the piano would stop at each floor, to be strung and to receive its action and keys, until reaching the warerooms.

The company continued as a leading piano manufacturer throughout the 19th century. In the early 20th century, however, the piano business suffered badly as new forms of entertainment (the Victrola, radio, and movie houses) challenged the piano's popularity. About 1928 manufacturing operations were transferred to Rochester, New York, and the Tremont Street factory was subdivided for commercial and industrial users. In 1973–74 the building was converted to the Piano-Craft Guild, 174 apartments plus working and exhibition areas, specifically designed for, and limited to, musicians, artists, and craftsmen.

The construction of the Chickering factory in the South End represented a movement away from the industry's old center on upper Tremont and Washington streets (where the showrooms remained) to the new filled land of the South End. By the 1860s the piano industry in the South End, with eleven separate firms, had become the largest single manufacturing industry in Boston, and much of its labor, especially German and Swedish craftsmen, came eventually to settle in that part of the city.

526   Smith American Organ Company/George Frost Company, garter m'f'y

551 Tremont Street

BOSTON SOUTH
^{3}29280.^{46}89850

The oldest organ factory in Boston was built in 1864 by Samuel D. and Henry W. Smith. Henry Smith (not, apparently, the melodeon manufacturer of the same name in Townsend) was credited, in 1885, with being "the first to make [reed] organs on the plan now generally adopted," and the company's success in the 1860s and 1870s prompted numerous imitators, including at least two Boston firms founded by former Smith employees.

Samuel and Henry Smith were cousins, both born in Enfield, Massachusetts, in 1830. In 1852 they came to Boston, establishing a melodeon factory on Washington Street. Melodeons (small, cased reed organs) were then reaching the height of their popularity, and S.D. & H.W. Smith, as the firm was styled, carried on a successful business. The experience must have prompted the firm to try larger models. The cabinet or parlor organ was introduced in 1861 by a Boston firm, possibly the Smiths, and in 1864 the company constructed a brick factory on Tremont Street. Originally the building had a fifth or attic floor beneath a mansard roof, but this was removed after a disastrous fire in 1885 (see figure 9). As reported by an insurance survey in 1878, the basement housed packing, storage, and drying rooms; the first floor, offices and warerooms; the second, finishing and tuning; on the third, the actions were set up and installed; and the fourth housed the reed, machine, and bellows rooms and, after the fire, the finishing and tuning that had previously been conducted in the attic. The wooden cases were constructed in a second plant on Albany Street (**527**). In 1885 the output of the plant was 150 instruments per week, and employment ranged from 200 to 400 hands. Instruments were made in twenty different styles, for "students, churches, professionals, chapels, home, and public purposes."

The company's history is in many respects paralleled by the more famous Mason & Hamlin Company, which like the Smiths' started as a melodeon manufacturer in Boston in 1854, graduated in the 1860s to cabinet organs, and in the 1880s added pianos to their line of organs. The Smith piano, styled "the Regal" and introduced in 1884, was based on a new method of insulating the vibrating body of the piano from the case itself. The company's name was changed to the Smith American Organ & Piano Company to reflect this new product. The Regal was not a success, though, and in 1892 the building was sold to George Frost & Company, a manufacturer of garters.

The garter had been patented in 1878 by F. Barton Brown, who assigned the right to manufacture the item to the George Frost Company of Boston. The company prospered, and after several moves to successively larger quarters it took over the old organ factory, making a five-story addition to the rear in 1906. By 1930 the firm employed 400 workers. "Boston Garters" for men and "Velvet Grip" hose supporters for women and children were internationally known. Both products eventually fell victim to changing tastes. Though the company maintained a Boston office through the 1950s, the factory was sold in the late 1940s to the Commercial Flower Exchange, which occupied it until 1969.

Adjoining the organ factory is the 1884 "Cyclorama," built to house a 400-foot Battle of Gettysburg panorama and altered to its present form in 1922 by the Boston Flower Exchange. Today both the Cyclorama and Smith's American Organ factory house units of the Boston Center for the Arts, a nonprofit umbrella organization providing studios, offices, and theater space for a wide variety of resident artists and groups.

527   Smith American Organ Company: case factory

BOSTON SOUTH

615 Albany Street ^{3}29480.^{46}89010

One indication of the size of the business conducted by the Smith American Organ Company is the existence of two separate substantial factories operated in tandem. Most of the other Boston organ and piano firms either contracted with outside firms for their cases or else constructed independent shops close to the source of raw material.

The Smith case factory was probably built in the 1860s on the South Bay waterfront to take advantage of the local lumber wharves and yards. Like the parent plant on Tremont Street before 1885, the four-story brick plant on Albany Street includes a fifth attic story beneath a mansard roof. Approximately 38×75 feet in plan, the building occupies only part of the block. An apparently contemporaneous section, 75×100 feet, occupied originally by the carpenters Cummings & Carlisle, was taken down in 1938. Today the case factory houses a research laboratory.

528   New England Organ Company

BOSTON SOUTH

46 Wareham Street ^{3}29670.^{46}89260

The popularity of the cabinet or parlor organ in the 1870s provided a strong incentive for the establishment of rival concerns. George T. McLaughlin and Thomas F. Scanlan had been employed by the Smith American Organ Company for seven or eight years when they decided in 1871 to organize the New England Organ Company. Their first factory was located at 53 Wareham Street, but about 1876 the firm moved across the street to a new three-story brick factory recently completed by John J. McNutt, whose own Novelty Wood Works (**518**) was located on the property immediately adjacent. The new factory, which McNutt leased to the organ company, features cast-iron window lintels with floral scrolls in negative relief. The basement housed the dry room and woodworking machinery, and offices occupied the first floor. Movements were made on the second floor, and the wooden cases were made on both floors. On the third floor the organs were varnished, polished, and then tuned.

The rising favor of pianos over organs must have attracted Thomas Scanlan's attention, for in 1881 he sold his interest to McLaughlin and left to form the New England Piano Company with a factory in Roxbury (**000**). Under McLaughlin, the New England Organ Company continued to manufacture organs for another decade. The prosperity of the business in the mid-1880s induced the firm to add an attic story to the building, beneath a mansard roof. This floor, devoted to regulating and finishing, no longer exists. The factory was closed about 1892, and McLaughlin eventually rejoined Scanlan at the New England Piano Company. Since the 1890s the Wareham Street factory has housed a variety of woodworking and furniture shops. Today it is occupied by an importer and distributor of quality foods.

529   Rogers Upright Piano Company ("Bacon's Building")

BOSTON SOUTH

486–498 Harrison Avenue ^{3}29780.^{46}89610

The adaptation of the overstrung scale and full iron frame to the upright piano after 1860 made the instrument much more acceptable to prospective buyers. In addition, the fact that an upright required much less space than a square or grand piano made it a favorite choice in American cities. The square piano, introduced as a more compact alternative to the grand, had been a favorite of Boston piano makers since the 1790s. By 1880 its place in the home had been largely usurped by the upright.

Because of the position of its keys in relation to its strings, the upright's key movement is complicated, and its design attracted the attention of many piano builders. Among them was Charles E. Rogers, who in 1872 patented a new piano action. With real estate entrepreneur Charles H. Bacon (1827–1906) as president and the founder of the Boston Music School, Benjamin F. Baker (1811–1889), as treasurer, the Rogers Upright Piano Company was formed in 1875. The existing factory on Harrison Avenue was constructed that year.

Rogers appears to have been connected with the firm for only a short time, going on to start the piano firms of Rogers & [Frank] Bacon and then the Charles E. Rogers Piano Company. For a few years

Rogers Upright prospered, but about 1878 the company fell on hard times. About 1880 the firm was reorganized as the B. F. Baker Upright Piano Company, and it continued to manufacture pianos under that name for most of the decade. Baker, however, was a music teacher and spent most of his time in Chicago. "Of his responsibility and reliability," the credit bureau wrote, "there are widely differing opinions, some regarding him as an honest man of very moderate means, and others maintaining that he is a sharp old schemer, worth upwards of $20,000 but which for good reasons he keeps in unattachable form. . . ." The company was wound up after Baker's death in 1889. For many years thereafter the building housed smaller woodworking industries, including makers of piano cases and doors and sashes.

A central passageway through the four-story brick structure connects Harrison Avenue with a lumber storage area to the rear of the building. Above the passage a granite plaque carries the legend "Bacon's Building."

530   Emerson Piano Company: Randolph Street Factory

BOSTON SOUTH

520–524 Harrison Avenue   [3]29730.[46]89560

William P. Emerson (1820–1871) was born in Boston. He began building pianos in 1849, though at the start it was with "perhaps more business acumen than mechanical talent or artistic inclination," the industry's historian has written. Although Emerson did a good business in low-priced pianos, it was not until he engaged Charles E. Briggs in 1854 that the Emerson piano began to develop as a quality instrument. After Emerson's death in 1871, the business came into the possession of William Moore. At the time the factory was located at the corner of Albany and Wareham streets (later the site of the Everett Piano Company [**532**]). The 1866 factory, built by J. J. McNutt, was destroyed by fire in December 1878. Although Moore rebuilt the following spring, he sold out less than two months later, to four of his employees, with Patrick H. Powers as president.

The new brick factory (which no longer survives), 65 × 300 feet in size, was located on Randolph Street. In 1882 the firm added the existing brick office and wing at the corner of Harrison Avenue. The five-story structure features a mansard roof and central tower over an open passageway through the building. In 1883 the company employed 200 hands and produced 80 pianos a week.

The company remained on Randolph Street until 1892 when a new plant on Waltham Street was opened (**531**). Subsequently the building housed the A. M. McPhail Piano Company and, from about 1899 to 1910, was the first home of the Hub Hosiery Mills (**000**). Since then the building has housed a series of smaller firms, including contractors, upholsterers, and woodworkers

531   Emerson Piano Company: Waltham Street Factory

560 Harrison Avenue

BOSTON SOUTH
^{3}29630.^{46}89460

Between 1879 and 1890 the business of the Emerson Piano Company expanded significantly. The company established branch stores in New York and Chicago, with sales agencies throughout Europe and America. In 1891 the company built a new brick factory at the corner of Waltham Street and Harrison Avenue, about 400 feet west of their earlier factory. Shortly after its completion, the company described it as "one of the largest and most completely equipped establishments for the manufacture of pianos in the world." The brick factory was between six and seven stories in height and 65 feet deep, with lumber yards and brick dryhouses in the rear. The builder and architect was Alonzo S. Drisko (1829–1914), a native of Addison, Maine, who had come to Boston in 1850 and had constructed a number of large buildings. In the 1880s he had established a shop in the Reed Block (**521**).

Three hundred workmen were employed in the new plant, and its maximum capacity was 125–150 pianos per week. The company remained here until about 1922, when it moved briefly into the old Everett Piano Company building on Albany Street (**532**). In 1923 the firm moved to Norwalk, Ohio. Mason & Hamlin manufactured pianos here for about four years after Emerson left. About 1927 the building was subdivided and since then has housed a large variety of commercial and light industries.

532   Everett Piano Company

495–527 Albany Street

BOSTON SOUTH
^{3}29730.^{46}89240

The piano industry reached its peak in Boston about 1890. In that year 29 separate factories employed nearly 2,000 workers. One of the most recent was the Everett Piano Company, a subsidiary of an Ohio firm, the Cincinnati-based John Church Company, which had been established in 1859. Frank A. Lee joined the Church Company in 1883, and in November of that year the Everett Piano Company was started in Boston through his efforts. Church chose the name

Everett for its "euphonious clearness. . . . as easy to remember as it is easy to spell."

Until 1886 the company was located in a factory on Federal Street, but in that year they purchased the land formerly occupied by the Emerson Piano factory, which had burned in 1878 (see **530**). The existing five-story brick factory was begun in 1887. The southern portion of the 300-foot-long building was completed that year, and the northern portion was completed by 1902. Architect for the piano company was Samuel Dudley Kelley (1848–1938), a native of Yarmouth, Massachusetts, who had moved to Boston thirteen years before.

By the early 20th century Everett concert grands were used by many of the world's leading virtuosos, the company claimed. After 1910, as the commercial popularity of the piano waned, the fortunes of many of the piano companies declined. The Everett factory closed its doors about 1918. In the early 1920s the Emerson Piano Company was located here before moving to Ohio. Since then the plant has served as headquarters for a variety of woodworking, clothing, and building supply firms.

533   West End Street Railway: Central Power Station

BOSTON SOUTH
540 Harrison Avenue ^{3}29760.^{46}89480

One of the incentives that attracted the woodworking and piano industries to the South End also attracted the West End Street Railway: ready access to the coal wharves along Albany Street.

The West End's new electric street-railway service, supplied from the small Allston generating station (**000**) beginning in 1889, was an immediate success. Less than ten months after the lines were energized, the West End management broke ground for a new Central Power Station between Harrison Avenue and Albany Street. The site was the old Hinkley Locomotive Works, and until 1941, when it was replaced by the present bus garage, the locomotive machine shop was used for repair and office purposes. Designed by William G. Preston, the new station was billed as "the largest electric powerhouse in the world" (figure 10). Completed in 1892, the plant included an engine room of 176 × 180 feet and an adjoining boiler room. Though the engine room was set well back from Harrison Avenue, so that it could have been doubled in size, only the boilerhouse, extending to the rear, was later enlarged, to its present 84 × 225 feet.

The chief engineer for the company and the individual most responsible for the power station was Frederick S. Pearson (1861–1915), until 1889 superintendent of the Somerville Electric Light Company (**000**) and later one of the leading electrical engineers in the country. Pearson obtained his first street railway experience with the West End, and during his tenure he solved many of the problems that arose in this first large electric railway system in the nation. By the time he left Boston to work for the Brooklyn Rapid Transit Company, the company had a reputation as the "largest and most complete system of electric street railways in the world."

The Harrison Avenue facade consists of three gable-roofed bays, each dominated by a broad semicircular window. Behind each of the two outside bays was a row of three triple-expansion Corliss engines, belt-connected to four rows of 500-hp Thompson-Houston generators in the center section. The 1890s, however, were a period of fundamental changes in the technology of the electric power industry. Pearson himself was the first in America to design (for Brooklyn) a large power station with direct-connected engine generators for street-railway service, and in 1896 the West End company connected its own generators directly to the engine shafts, making room for three new engines.

By 1904 the station had a capacity of 14,400 kilowatts, about 40% of the entire system's capacity. Use of the station was discontinued with the construction of the new alternating-current central station in South Boston in 1911 (**000**). Since that time the building has served successive transit authorities primarily as a maintenance facility. Though all generating equipment has been removed, its place taken by cable storage, the facility's original General Electric panel board is still in place, as are two large GE synchronous generators that were used until 1983.

534 Boston Transit Commission: Tremont Street Subway (Green Line)

Park Street to Bolyston Street

BOSTON SOUTH
^{3}30100.^{46}91180

By the early 1890s Boston had probably a greater number of radiating electric streetcar lines than any other city in the country, and by far the most electrified track mileage. The very extent of the service had led to a serious congestion problem. Most of the lines funneled into a narrow corridor of Boston streets, chiefly Tremont and Washington streets, which also carried a heavy traffic of wagons and carts. There had been proposals to construct underground or elevated railways, but the solution to the congestion problem, as was recognized in contemporary journals, was not to provide rapid transit but to facilitate traffic flow on certain existing routes within a small area about a mile long and a quarter-mile wide. Henry Whitney had proposed a tunnel in 1887, and in chartering the West End Street Railway that year the legislature had authorized the company to build one. Many of the details of the tunnel, as well as of the later elevated route, were first developed by George S. Rice, engineer for the short-lived Rapid Transit Commission (1891–1892).

The Boston Transit Commission was established in 1894 expressly to construct a streetcar tunnel, which would then be leased to the street railway company. The chief engineer appointed to the commission was Howard A. Carson (1842–1931), who had earlier been responsible for the design of the North Metropolitan Sewerage System (see **561**). As transit commission engineer, he would later be responsible for the East Boston subway tunnel (**536**), the Washington Street tunnel (**535**), and the Cambridge subway under Beacon Hill (**537**).

Construction was begun on the 1.8-mile cut-and-cover tunnel in March 1895 despite the vociferous objections of many who resented the subway's intrusion into the Common, feared for the safety of buildings along the route, or prophesied that passengers would be uncomfortable riding through "Stygian" caverns. The original subway, much of which is still in use today, ran from North Station through Haymarket, Scollay Square (now Government Center), and Park Street, to Boylston (figure 11). There the line diverged to connect with two major streetcar routes from the south and west, following Boylston and Tremont streets. The westerly branch rose to the surface at an incline in the Public Garden (replaced in 1914). The southerly route (unused and closed off since the 1960s) followed Tremont Street to its junction with Shawmut Avenue, where it met descending surface car tracks from these two streets.

Between Haymarket and Scollay Square, and between Park Street and Boylston, the tunnel was provided with four tracks; the remainder of the subway was double-tracked. Loop tracks were provided at Park Street, Scollay Square, and North Station. The first section of the subway, between Park Street and the Public Garden, opened on September 1, 1897, the southern branch a month later, and the final section from Park Street to North Station on September 3, 1898.

Many changes have been made since 1898. Between 1901 and 1908, when the Washington Street tunnel was completed, Main Line Elevated cars were routed through the subway; a lower level (Park Street Under) was constructed in 1909–1912 when the Cambridge Subway was built. The opening of the Lechmere Viaduct (**000**) and elevated structure in

1912 provided surface cars from Cambridge and Somerville with a high-speed connection to the Tremont Street Subway. In 1912–1914 the subway was extended along Boylston and Beacon streets to Kenmore Square, and a branch was built along Huntington Avenue to Symphony Hall in 1937–1941. When Government Center was constructed in the early 1960s, the tunnel was relocated between Scollay Square and Haymarket and new stations were built. Since the redecoration of Park Street Station in 1977, only the Boylston Station retains its original character. The southern branch to Shawmut Avenue also remains in place, though unused. Also original to the subway are the classical granite kiosks that shelter the station stairways at Park Street and Boylston. The original designs for the kiosks were prepared by city architect Edmund M. Wheelwright (1854–1912), but his plans were considerably reduced by the Transit Commission to a set of unconnected stone structures that relate poorly to their surroundings (a fact that was recognized by contemporary critics).

The construction of the Tremont Street Subway, the first transit tunnel in the United States and the fifth in the world, represented the first phase of the transition of an extensive street-railway network into a rapid transit system, most of which occurred in the two decades 1898–1918. This was not, however, a rapid transit subway like the later Cambridge Subway (today's Red Line); it was a tunnel for surface cars, and today's Green Line remains essentially a streetcar line, by contrast with the later Subway or Main Line Elevated Orange Line. The subway was designated a National Historic Landmark in 1964 and a National Historic Civil Engineering Landmark in 1978.

535   Boston Transit Commission: Washington Street Tunnel (Orange Line)

Haymarket to Essex Street

BOSTON SOUTH
^{3}30440.^{46}91260

The same legislation that established the Boston Transit Commission to build the Tremont Street Subway also chartered the Boston Elevated Railway Company to build an elevated rapid transit line on the model outlined by the Rapid Transit Commission in 1892. Unable to raise the necessary capital, the company's original investors sold the charter to a syndicate headed by New York investment banker J. Pierpont Morgan in 1895. After a turbulent proxy fight, the Elevated gained control of the West End Street Railway in 1897, leasing it for a term of 25 years.

The Main Line Elevated, connecting Sullivan Square in Charlestown and Dudley Station in Roxbury (**000**), was started in 1899 and opened in June 1901. The Atlantic Avenue loop (see **539**) opened two months later, and in 1909 the route's southern end was extended to Forest Hills. The route was double-tracked throughout. Of the seven original elevated stations, the terminal at Sullivan Square was the most elaborate, featuring a great trainshed sheltering the loop tracks and surface-car ramps to the elevated level to permit cross-platform transfers. Chief engineer for the Elevated and the designer of most of its route was George A. Kimball (1850–1912). The seven original elevated stations formed the subject of a design competition in 1898, and the winner was Alexander Wadsworth Longfellow (1854–1934), nephew of the poet and a draftsman under H. H. Richardson in the 1880s. Of Longfellow's original Gothic stations, executed in copper, only the Northampton Street Station survives unaltered, and that will be demolished with the remaining Elevated structure when the new Southwest Corridor line is completed. "Tower C," the two-story copper-sheathed interlocking tower which stood at Keany Square, was moved in 1975 to the Seashore Trolley Museum in Kennebunkport, Maine.

The Elevated's original route through downtown Boston passed through the Tremont Street Subway, utilizing the Shawmut Avenue ramp and outer tracks as far as North Station. Because this displaced much of the surface-car traffic, the Transit Commission soon began planning a separate downtown route that would run parallel to the subway. Like the two earlier tunnels built by the commission and leased to the Elevated, the tunnel was the work of the commission's chief engineer, Howard Carson. Begun in the fall of 1904 and completed four years later, the new tunnel was double-tracked throughout its 6,100-foot length. For much of its route it followed Washington Street, and on account of the narrowness and crookedness of the street, the station platforms had to be staggered, those for the north and southbound traffic not being opposite one another.

Although most of the station entrances were situated in existing buildings, those at Adams Square (now demolished) and Milk Street (extant) were given cast-concrete stairway roofs with curved, sloping surfaces. Glass sidewalk lights set in the concrete provided illumination to the stairs. The Art Nouveau entrances were cast from a single mold by the Aberthaw Construction Company. The architectural treatment of the station interiors was under the direction of Robert S. Peabody (1845–1917) of the firm of Peabody & Stearns. Of the original four stations in the tunnel, only those at Washington and Milk streets show any of the original tile work. North of State Street the tunnel was completely relocated in the 1960s in connection with the construction of Government Center. In 1975 the tunnel was extended north beyond North Station under the Charles River, rising to the surface on a new alignment west of the line's old station at City Square.

536 Boston Transit Commission: East Boston Tunnel (Blue Line)

BOSTON SOUTH

Court Street to Maverick Square, East Boston   ³31450.⁴⁶91700

Another provision of the 1894 legislation establishing the Boston Transit Commission provided for the construction of a trolley tunnel beneath Boston Harbor that would link the streetcar tracks of East Boston with those of the Tremont Street Subway. The East Boston Tunnel was the second underwater tunnel to be completed in the United States, following the Saint Clair Tunnel at Port Huron, Michigan, which opened in 1890. Including approaches, the tunnel was 7,500 feet long, of which 2,700 feet were under water. The 23-foot-diameter single-tube construction also made this the widest such tunnel yet constructed. Its unprecedented dimensions and its successful use of concrete as a tunnel lining brought considerable notice in contemporary engineering periodicals.

Before designing the structure, the Transit Commission's chief engineer Howard Carson inspected various European transit systems. Transit tunnels in both London and Glasgow employed twin tubes, each carrying a single track. For both the Tremont Street Subway and the East Boston Tunnel, Carson chose to depart from this model, opting instead for a single, wider tube carrying two electric railroad tracks. Construction of the tunnel was carried out using an iron roof shield running upon side walls previously built in small drifts, the bulk of the excavation being performed later under the protection of the shield. Most earlier tunnels had been lined with cast-iron segments. Possibly reflecting Carson's design experience with the Metropolitan Sewerage Board, the East Boston Tunnel was lined with a monolithic layer of concrete, 33 inches thick.

The tunnel opened for service on December 30, 1904, after four and a half years of construction. The original endpoints of the tunnel were at Maverick Square, where the tracks rose to the surface, and at Court Street, a few feet distant from the Scollay Square Station. A pedestrian passageway linked the two latter stations. Intermediate stops were built at Atlantic Avenue (now "Aquarium") and Devonshire Street (now "State").

Direct connection was never made to Scollay Square. Instead, in 1916 the tunnel was extended another 2,600 feet to Bowdoin Square, where an underground station, a loop, and a surface incline to Cambridge Street were provided. In the extension, the original tunnel was lowered to pass beneath Scollay Square Station (creating "Scollay Under"), and the Court Street Station was abandoned.

Until 1924 the tunnel was used only by streetcars. The surface incline at Bowdoin Square allowed a connection with Cambridge streetcar tracks passing along Cambridge Street and over the Longfellow Bridge. This created a direct streetcar route between Cambridge and East Boston. The link also provided transit cars of the Blue Line (to use the modern terminology) direct access to the Red Line's Eliot Street repair shops, west of Harvard Square, the Blue Line having no shops of its own.

In 1924 streetcar operation was replaced by third-rail rapid-transit service. Passenger service was discontinued beyond Bowdoin, but trains continued to be run in the late hours of the evening to the Eliot Street shops through the Red Line's Cambridge Tunnel. Not until the construction of the Blue Line's new Orient Heights shops in 1952—and the simultaneous extension of passenger service from Maverick to Orient Heights—was the Cambridge Street incline finally closed permanently.

537 Boston Transit Commission: Beacon Hill Tunnel (Red Line)

Park Street to Longfellow Bridge

BOSTON SOUTH

^{3}30100.^{46}91180

The Beacon Hill Tunnel, constructed between 1909 and 1911, was an extension of the Cambridge Subway (see **000**) into Boston Proper, the two sections being connected by a surface line on the Longfellow Bridge (**000**) and a short elevated line to the mouth of the tunnel. The original double-bore tunnel was 2,488 feet in length including the 350-foot station "Park Street Under," constructed beneath the Park Street Station of the original subway. About 60% of the tunnel was constructed using a roof shield, a semicircular steel enclosure roughly three-quarters the size of the tunnel bore being excavated. The remainder of the tunnel, including the station and its approach, was constructed by hand methods from three shafts opened on the Common. The chief engineer for this project, as for the three previous tunnels built by the Transit Commission, was Howard Carson.

The new station and tunnel were opened for service in March 1912. The tunnel was extended to South Station in 1916, to Broadway in South Boston a year later, and to Andrew Square in 1918. The Charles Street Station, beyond the tunnel's west end, was opened in February 1932 to accommodate the Massachusetts General Hospital. Stations at Washington Street and South Station still retain the line's original wooden escalators, manufactured by the Reno Inclined Elevator Company of New York.

538   South Station

BOSTON SOUTH

Dewey Square ^{3}30660.^{46}90660

One of the recommendations of the Rapid Transit Commission in 1892 (see **534**) was the consolidation of existing railroad terminals into two union stations, North and South. North Station, built by the Boston & Maine, was the first to be constructed (**551**). South Station was constructed between 1896 and 1899.

Prior to 1899, each of the railroads from the west and south operated its own passenger and freight terminal. The Boston & Providence maintained a high Victorian brick and stone terminal at Park Square; the Boston & Albany and Old Colony roads operated parallel brick depots terminating at Kneeland Street. The New York & New England Railroad had a wooden passenger depot on the present site of South Station at Dewey Square, but its orientation was parallel to Summer Street, and its rail lines came in from the east, over Fort Point Channel from South Boston. In 1896 the railroad companies organized the Boston Terminal Company to construct and maintain a union passenger station. The new terminal, which opened on January 1, 1899, successfully consolidated the lines of the four railroads into one trainshed. For many years this was the nation's largest and busiest railroad station.

Architect for the station was the prominent Boston firm of Shepley, Rutan & Coolidge, with George B. Francis as resident engineer. The terminal featured a number of innovative features. South Station was the first major American railroad station designed in the Beaux Arts style made popular by the 1893 World's Columbian Exposition in Chicago and was inspired by Charles B. Atwood's terminal station for the exposition. The trainshed, designed by J. R. Worcester, was at 570 feet the second widest in the world after one in St. Louis. The station's double-deck plan, with long-distance and suburban passenger services separated into two levels, predated Grand Central Terminal's use of this plan by fourteen years. Other features included baggage handling removed from the main platform and a loop-track arrangement designed to expedite the anticipated increase in passenger service.

The original U-shaped station extended 2,189 feet along Atlantic and Dorchester avenues and Summer Street, with the five-story base of the U serving as the main station building. Since its construction, however, the station has been dramatically altered. In 1930, as a result of the weakening effect of air pollutants, the steel and glass trainshed was dismantled. In the late 1960s and early 1970s, much of the eastern portion of the yard, the western Atlantic Avenue wing, and part of the Summer Street waiting room were demolished. The five-story granite headhouse, the station's most dramatic architectural feature, still survives.

As originally designed, the station had 28 platform tracks, handling, in 1899, 737 daily trains. Passenger service peaked in 1945, with 46 million users. By the mid-1960s this figure had shrunk to 4.5 million passengers. In connection with the Northeast Corridor Improvement Project, the station is being rehabilitated in line with the reduced demand. The reconstructed terminal layout will have 11 platform tracks on a new alignment; the headhouse will be rehabilitated and a new concourse constructed. In addition, six levels of air rights will be developed by the Massachusetts Bay Transportation Authority and the Boston Redevelopment Authority. The MBTA plans a three-level transportation center and the BRA a High Technology Center with space for offices, a hotel, and light industry. The phased development is planned to be completed in 1987.

539   Boston Elevated Railway: Lincoln Wharf Power Station
BOSTON SOUTH
365 Commercial Street   ³31100.⁴⁶92060

Designed to connect the new North and South stations, the Boston Elevated's Atlantic Avenue Branch opened in August 1901, two months after the Elevated's Main Line (see **535**). The Atlantic Avenue loop left the Main Line near where the latter today crosses the Massachusetts Turnpike, then followed successively Harrison Avenue, Beach Street, Atlantic Avenue, and Commercial Street to the Charlestown Bridge (**000**), where it again met up again with the El. A station at Rowe's Wharf connected with the ferry of the Boston, Revere Beach & Lynn Railroad, a major source of traffic; and when the ferry stopped running in 1938, the operation of the Atlantic Avenue loop ceased as well. The structure was demolished in 1942. (Part of its route along Atlantic

Avenue was followed by a later elevated structure, today's Fitzgerald Expressway, built between 1954 and 1959.)

The chief monument to the Atlantic Avenue loop, and its only surviving structure, is the Lincoln Wharf Power Station, constructed in 1901 to the designs of the Elevated's chief engineer, George A. Kimball. By 1901 seven power plants supplied direct current for the surface cars of the Elevated's system. All had been built by the El's predecessor, the West End Street Railway (**533**), and they were not adequate to the demands of the new elevated line. The new Lincoln Wharf station, though its chief function was to supply the elevated lines, also supplied power to the surface lines. The station was originally equipped with three vertical cross-compound condensing engines, direct-connected to three 2,700-kilowatt generators. At the time of their installation, these were the largest direct-current railway generators yet constructed. The combined capacity of the plant by 1904 was 8,100 kw, about 22% of the system's capacity.

The original building was designed by the mechanical and electrical engineers Sheaff & Jaastad of Boston. The building features stepped gables and a slate roof with clerestory monitor and dormers. The existing three-bay classical facade was added in 1907, when the station was expanded to meet new power demands on the system. Under the direction of the Stone & Webster Engineering Corporation, extensions aggregating 12,000 kw were planned for the Charlestown, Harvard, and Lincoln power stations. At Lincoln Wharf, two 2,700-kw units, of the type installed in 1901, were added to the plant. The chief ornament of the neoclassical addition is a great bronze eagle near the roof line of the Commercial Street facade.

Lincoln Wharf was later entirely re-equipped for alternating-current generation and remained in use long after the other stations had been discontinued.

Today the building is empty, and a proposal has been made to convert the structure into 150 condominium units for area residents. A large wood-frame coal pocket on the harbor side of the building (one of two originally on the site) could find use as a recreational center and harbor fire-fighting facility.

540   Walter M. Lowney Company Chocolate Factory

BOSTON SOUTH

427–439 Commercial Street ^{3}30920.^{46}92400

The oldest of several confectionery plants in the North End was that built for the Walter M. Lowney Company in 1896. The company's founder and namesake was born in Sebec, Maine, in 1856. In 1883, at the age of 27, Lowney began manufacturing chocolate bonbons at 89 South Street. The business was so successful that after a year and a half he employed 50 people. The firm was incorporated in 1890, and in 1893 the company erected its own building at the Chicago World's Fair. In 1898 the firm moved into new quarters at the corner of Commercial and Hanover streets. The five-story brick block, including a steam and refrigerating plant, was designed by the Boston engineering firm of Dean & Main. The factory was expanded to the rear in 1901, and the following year a paper box factory was established.

The company is credited with initiating and marketing packaged candy in a large way, and "it is probable," Orra Stone wrote in 1930, "that the present common practice of cooling chocolate dipping and chocolate packing rooms was first employed by this company." The company had a boom period in the early 20th century. In 1903 Lowney built a large chocolate and cocoa works in Mansfield, Massachusetts, and another in Montreal in 1906. Lowney himself moved to Mansfield, where he oversaw the establishment of employee housing, a model dairy farm (for the chocolate works), and various social amenities. The company was absorbed by another confectionery firm, Candy Brands, Inc., about 1931, ten years after the founder's death. Since World War II the complex has housed the U.S. Coast Guard, which has made the 11-building facility the agency's New England Support Center.

541   Hazen Confectionery Company/Touraine Company, confectioners

119–127 North Washington Street

BOSTON SOUTH

^{3}30480.^{46}92200

The Hazen Confectionery Company was established about 1903 by James W. Hazen, son of the well-known Cambridge confectioner Daniel M. Hazen. For several years the younger Hazen had been secretary-treasurer of the Kennedy Bakery in Cambridge (**000**), but in 1903 Hazen erected the existing five-story brick commercial building on North Washington Street, to the designs of Boston architects Walter T. Winslow and Henry F. Bigelow. The company was particularly known for their chocolates, and "Hazen's Oxford Chocolates" were frequently advertised in the first decade of the century.

Hazen was the first of three confectioners in as many decades to occupy the building. After the firm closed, about 1912, its place was taken by another candy manufacturer, the Loose-Wiles Company, organized only a year or so earlier by the St. Louis, Missouri, founders of the Loose-Wiles Biscuit Company, whose bakery was nearby on Causeway Street (see **543**). About 1923 the Touraine Company moved into the candy factory. The company had been established about 1907 by Harry B. Duane, and from about 1908 to 1922 the firm was located at 251 Causeway Street, near North Station. In 1929 the company employed 300 men and women. The Touraine Company remained on North Washington Street until about 1933, when it moved to Cambridge (**000**). Since then the first floor has housed a succession of food machinery suppliers, with the upper floors used for smaller wholesale firms. The building was rehabilitated for office space on the upper floors in 1978.

542   W. F. Schrafft & Sons, confectioners

160 North Washington Street   [3]30370.[46]92390

A third confectioner to build in the North End in this period was William F. Schrafft (1823–1906). Schrafft was a native of Bavaria who came to New York as a political refugee about 1850. In 1860 or 1865 he opened a small candy manufacturing business in Boston. When new refineries and the introduction of new equipment led to a fall in the price of sugar, Schrafft's business expanded with the industry. In 1895 Schrafft's sons, William E. and George F., were taken into the business. With the addition of Frank G. Shattuck, a successful confectionery salesman, the company embarked on a new period of expansion. In 1897 they opened a retail candy store in New York City, and in 1898 they began to serve lunches there. By 1928 there were 29 Schrafft candy and luncheon shops in New York City, 4 in Boston, and 1 in Syracuse. In conjunction with this expansion, Schrafft undertook a new eight-story candy factory on North Washington Street, adjacent to the recently completed Charlestown Bridge (**000**). This building was completed in 1906, the year of W. F. Schrafft's death. The baroque, panel-brick design of the Charles River facade reflects, perhaps unconsciously, the founder's Bavarian heritage. Details include oculi, fanciful Victorian parapets, and decorative brick patterns. In 1928 the company moved to Charlestown (see **000**), and the building was converted to loft and office space, a pattern it retains today.

543   Austin Biscuit Company/Loose-Wiles Biscuit Company

BOSTON SOUTH

226 Causeway Street ^{3}30380.^{46}92330

In 1907 C. F. Austin & Company constructed a six-story brick bakery on the lot adjoining the Schrafft plant. The business had been established on the Boston waterfront in 1825 by Thomas Austin (1789–1864), a provision merchant from Plymouth. Under the founder's son Charles, the firm expanded in the 1860s, erecting in Chelsea what became the largest cracker bakery in the Boston area (see **000**).In the early 20th century the company divided its business between dog biscuits, which continued to be produced in the Chelsea plant, and crackers, for which the company erected the present 106 × 313 foot brick structure on Causeway Street. The building was designed by the Boston firm of Codman & Despradelle.

The bakery opened in 1908. In March 1909 the company was acquired by the Loose-Wiles Biscuit Company, a firm established in St. Louis, Missouri, in 1902 by Joseph and Jacob Loose. Its chief products were known nationwide as "Sunshine Biscuits." The Boston plant originated the "Sunshine Hydrox" biscuit as well as the firm's popular line of English-style biscuits. By 1930 the firm operated ten factories across the country and owned 129 retail agencies. The Boston plant alone employed 1,000 hands. The firm continued to operate the bakery until the mid-1940s. Since about 1952 the building has been a bakery for Stop & Shop, Inc., a Boston-area grocery chain.

544   United Candy Company

BOSTON SOUTH

325 North Street ^{3}31030.^{46}92120

In 1912 the United Drug Company (**000**) built a large confectionery plant in the North End to supply its growing chain of Rexall and Liggett drugstores across the country. Known as the United Candy Company, the firm built an eight-story plant, 100 feet high, of modern "fire-proof construction." In the early 1940s the confectionery operations were consolidated in the main plant at Leon Street, Roxbury, and for a number of years the North End building remained vacant. Today, its openings bricked in, the building serves as a cold-storage facility.

545 Prince Macaroni Manufacturing Company

BOSTON SOUTH

43–63 Atlantic Avenue
^{3}31040.^{46}91900

The Prince Macaroni Manufacturing Company was incorporated in 1917 by Gaetano LaMarca, a native of Villa Rosa, Italy, who had arrived in Boston in 1901 with his brothers Michele and Giuseppe. For a number of years the LaMarca Brothers operated a bread store at 390 Hanover Street, and in 1912 Gaetano and two associates set up a macaroni factory in a small store on Prince Street.

In 1917 the Prince Macaroni Manufacturing Company erected the existing eight-story reinforced-concrete macaroni factory, designed by consulting engineer Burtis S. Brown of Boston. The building was originally 98 feet high. By the late 1920s the firm employed 125 men and women.

The company moved to Lowell in 1939, where it has since become a leading manufacturer of macaroni products. From 1940 until the mid-1960s the Boston plant housed a variety of smaller tenants. Among its users were a grocery wholesaler and, for over a decade, the Milano Re-Tanning Company, leather tanners. In 1966 the building became one of the first rehabilitation projects in Boston to adapt an industrial building to residential use. Architects for the renovation were Anderson Notter Associates of Boston, who created 42 apartments, two levels of enclosed tenant parking, and a level of office space. Two and a half stories were added to the building's height, and concrete balconies were added to the building's waterfront facade. Completed in May 1968, the renovation served as an important catalyst for other redevelopment projects along Boston's waterfront.

546 Edison Electric Illuminating Company: Salem Street Station, No. 30

BOSTON SOUTH

136 Salem Street
^{3}30700.^{46}92160

Since 1898 the Edison Electric Illuminating Company (now Boston Edison) has maintained parallel distribution systems for alternating and direct current to meet the requirements of its various customers. Because DC is less efficient than AC, it requires more and larger structures to provide electricity for local consumption. Between 1896 and 1930 the Edison company (see **515**) built approximately sixteen local DC substations within Boston Proper. Of these only five remain, and none of these serve the purpose for which they were built.

The earliest substation still remaining is the Salem Street Station (figure 12). Five and a half stories in height, the brick building with decorative brick bands and a rounded corner was designed by the firm's Boston architects, Winslow, Bigelow & Wadsworth.

The station entered service on October 23, 1909 to supply the North End territory formerly served by a similar substation on North Street. Rather than using the new rotary converters, which the company found still unreliable, the earliest stations used motor-generator sets to convert the 4,600-volt AC service from the main L Street generating station to 250-volt local DC service.

Although its DC service was discontinued in November 1957, the Salem Street facility continues to serve as an AC distribution substation, transforming 14,000 volts to 4,000-volt service for distribution to local customers in the North End and West End. The building's window openings were bricked over in 1963 as a precaution against vandalism.

547   Edison Electric Illuminating Company: Beacon Street Station, No. 49

687 Beacon Street

BOSTON SOUTH
^{3}27070.^{46}90330

The Kenmore Square area was the last section of Boston Proper to be developed. By 1916, when the Beacon Street substation was constructed, the area was experiencing a rapid commercial growth, particularly in automobile salesrooms, gasoline stations, garages, and related services. A herald of this growth was the construction of the Fenway Park stadium four years before.

Perhaps because of the few customers requiring DC service, the station was one of the first to be converted to exclusively AC distribution. In 1954 the station's remaining DC load was transferred to rectifiers in a nearby ground vault. Today, like the Salem Street substation, the building serves as a distribution point for the 4,000-volt local service.

The five-story brick and limestone building, designed by Bigelow & Wadsworth, is mainly classical in style, with a high rusticated first story dominated by the central round-arch steel door typical of the later Edison stations in Boston.

548   Edison Electric Illuminating Company: Chauncy Street Station, No. 21

BOSTON SOUTH

44 Chauncy Street   ³30300.⁴⁶90890

The Chauncy Street substation was completed in 1918, two years after the one at Kenmore Square. It was built to serve part of the expanding load of the downtown commercial and theater districts. The substation's unusual 145-foot, five-story height and 45-foot width reflects the scarcity of space in the area. For this prime location Wadsworth & Bigelow designed a windowless brick facade with a decorative vertical diaper pattern in raised brick, arranged in five bays. The top floor terminates the vertical bands in five round-arched panels ornamented with tile.

The first story, 46 feet in height, housed rotary converters (they had become more reliable since the Salem Street Station was constructed), transformers on two galleries above the main floor, and a 50-ton traveling crane above them. Entrance to the floor is gained through a single 20-foot arched steel door in the center of the brick facade. The second floor housed the operating room and switchboards; on the third floor were the buss compartments; and the fourth and fifth floors contained storage batteries, allowing the station a reserve supply of direct current for periods of peak demand.

The Chauncy Street Station was the last DC substation to be withdrawn from operation, shutting down in a recorded ceremony on November 10, 1977. The building was sold in 1983 to the owners of the adjoining Windsor Building.

549   Edison Electric Illuminating Company: Carver Street Station, No. 71

BOSTON SOUTH

70–74 Charles Street South (formerly Carver Street)   ³29770.⁴⁶90520

One of two DC substations built in 1924, Carver Street was put into operation on September 29, 1924. Like the Chauncy Street station, it features a blank brick facade divided into panels above a high arched central entrance. The station was converted to exclusively AC service in 1961. Today it is one of Boston Edison's five network stations transforming the utility's 115,000-volt supply to the 14,000-volt feeder network.

550   Edison Electric Illuminating Company: Cambridge Street Station, No. 72

BOSTON SOUTH

319 Cambridge Street ^{3}29500.^{46}91740

Five weeks after the Carver Street substation was energized, a new substation opened on Cambridge Street to serve the West End and Beacon Hill. Designed by Bigelow & Wadsworth, the 70-foot-high station originally featured a largely blank brick facade above a limestone-faced lower story; new window openings were inserted in 1983. A high round-arched central entrance displays elaborate wrought-iron grillwork.

When it opened in November 1924, the new substation was specially equipped for automatic operation. The first such automatic operation was recorded in 1926, a pioneer example of completely automatic 250-volt DC supply. The facility also represents one of the last enclosed substations built by the Edison company in Boston. By 1924 Boston Proper had been divided into twelve separate DC distribution districts, each served by its own substation. The introduction of the vacuum-tube rectifier, which changed AC to DC without requiring space-consuming rotating equipment, gradually eliminated the need for this expensive real estate. Rectifiers placed in underground vaults were introduced in Boston in 1932. The DC load of the Cambridge Street Station was transferred to a nearby street vault in 1968, and the building itself was later sold to the nearby Massachusetts Eye & Ear Infirmary, which converted the structure in 1984 into a medical office building.

Boston is one of the last cities in the country to maintain a DC distribution system. The city's economic stagnation in the 1950s and 1960s discouraged investment in new equipment such as elevator machinery, and today a substantial number of downtown Boston buildings still require both systems.

551   Boston & Maine Railroad: North Station

BOSTON SOUTH

100 Causeway Street ^{3}30150.^{46}92170

North Station, constructed in 1928, represents the peak of the Boston & Maine's development in the early 20th century, part of a major effort to recover those rail passengers who had started deserting the railroads in the 1920s for the automobile and the bus. The station was also the most visible public aspect of the company's vast program to consolidate the freight and passenger facilities of what had once been four separate and competing railroads: the Boston & Lowell, which entered Boston in 1835; the Boston & Maine (1845); the Fitchburg (1848); and the Eastern Railroad (1854).

Each line had built its own station on, or close to, Causeway Street. As late as 1893, each station was still being operated independently, though all but the Fitchburg had passed into Boston & Maine ownership. The original North Station, behind a hugh triumphal arch, opened in 1894, linking the Boston & Lowell and Fitchburg facilities with a new structure. Seven years later the Fitchburg, too, came into the possession of the B&M. Not until the late 1920s, however, was the company financially able to undertake the physical reorganization of either the four freight yards north of the Charles River (see **000**) or the four passenger facilities.

The new North Station was built as the central unit of an extensive terminal development project that included a coliseum and sports arena called the Boston Garden; a 500-room hotel, later the Madison (demolished in 1983); and a 13-story industrial building. The hotel was built on the site of the old Boston & Lowell station, and the North Station Industrial Building was constructed on the site of the old Fitchburg station. (The stones of the Fitchburg's gothic edifice were used in the new retaining walls along the river.) Architects for the new station were Fellheimer & Wagner of New York. The firm's art-deco design, reaching 550 feet along Causeway Street, has always been partially concealed behind the elevated transit structure that fronts it. Inside, a concourse extends nearly the width of the station, giving access to what originally were 23 tracks. Today all but 11 of these tracks have been paved over for parking. Above the concourse the railroad built a coliseum nearly identical in spatial configuration to Madison Square Garden in New York. It was to be operated, under lease from the railroad, by the Boston Madison Square Garden Corporation.

552 Boston & Maine Railroad: Electric Light & Power Station

BOSTON SOUTH

34 Minot Street at Nashua Street ^{3}29960.^{46}92270

In 1894, in conjunction with the Boston & Maine's construction of the first Union, or North, Station, the company built a large steam plant to heat the buildings and cars and to furnish power. The only available location was an unoccupied piece of land at the end of one of the brick freight houses of the old Boston & Lowell Railroad, perpendicular to Minot Street. (The freight houses, now demolished, occupied part of the site on which the state's Department of Public Works built its headquarters in 1932.) A portion of the end of one of the freight houses was incorporated into the new building. The two-story brick plant supplied steam to the old Lowell Station, at the corner of Causeway and Nashua streets, to the new Union Station, and to the cars on outgoing trains. Steam drove an air compressor for the operation of block signals in the yard. Steam-powered electric generators supplied electric arc lights in the train-house and yard and incandescent lamps in the rest of the buildings.

The railroad stopped using the building in 1928 when the existing North Station (**551**) was constructed. The property was acquired by the Edison Electric Illuminating Company as a district steam-heating plant to supply not only the new North Station and its associated buildings but much of the adjoining area as well. Today the Minot Street plant is linked to the main Kneeland Street Station (**554**) by an extensive series of steam mains. The plant has two boilers with a total capacity of 300,000 lb per hour, about a quarter the capacity of the Kneeland Street boilers. Fuel oil for the plant is delivered by an underground pipeline nearly six miles long linking the L Street Sation in South Boston (**000**) with the Mystic Station in Everett (**000**). One of Minot Street's chief customers is the Massachusetts General Hospital.

553   Boston & Maine Railroad: Charles River Bridges

BOSTON SOUTH

Charles River, north of North Station ^{3}29880.^{46}92590

Part of the extensive terminal improvement program by the Boston & Maine in the 1920s, and the last element to be completed, was the replacement and realignment of the railroad's crossings of the Charles River. The Boston & Lowell had become the first railroad in the United States to build a movable bridge when, in 1835, they had to figure out an efficient way to extend their tracks across the Charles River into Boston. The railroad's solution was a movable span with a horizontal swing, hinged at the corner of one end. A system of cables supported the free end of the span. The structure was the forerunner of the "jackknife" bridge, invented in 1849. (The last known example is still in service over the Mystic River. See **000**.) One by one, the three other railroads crossing the Charles adopted this solution (and later the jackknife design), which became a characteristic feature of the railroads north of Boston. Not until 1931 were the Charles River bridges replaced (they were then among the last examples left in the country). To the very end, the bridges were air- and steam-operated.

In 1931, after extensive filling and dredging, the channel of the Charles was relocated further away from North Station to allow the terminal tracks to converge into eight main leads. These were carried over the river on four new double-track structures in the form of single-leaf rolling-lift bascules, a design made famous by the Scherzer Rolling Lift Bridge Company of Chicago (**000**). These four were nearly identical, varying only in their length and the degree of their skew, two spans crossing the channel at a slightly greater skew than the others. Two were 87 feet in length and two 97 feet. Each span carried a single 629-ton overhead concrete counterweight operated by two electric motors; the motors were controlled from the second floor of the new signal and interlocking station, located nearby on the north side of the river. The bridges were designed by Keller & Harrington of Chicago, while the steelwork was fabricated and erected by the Phoenix Bridge Company of Phoenixville, Pennsylvania. Today only two of the bascule spans remain, the westernmost (Lifts 3 and 4) having been removed in 1961 after the railroad discontinued long-haul passenger service.

554   Edison Electric Illuminating Company: Kneeland Street Steam Heating Plant

155 Kneeland Street

BOSTON SOUTH

^{3}30430.^{46}90400

District steam heating, whereby a number of centrally located buildings are heated from a common steam plant, was introduced in the United States in 1881 in New York City. In Boston the Edison Electric Illuminating Company (**515**) was supplying steam to properties adjoining its electric generating stations as early as 1887. As the system expanded in the first decades of this century, the company leased small plants to supply downtown office buildings and later restaurants, department stores, hotels, theaters, candy manufacturers, clothing and hat manufacturers, and other businesses.

In 1922 the company adopted a definite expansion program. New steam mains were installed, for the first time linking all the steam heating plants then controlled by the company. In the late 1920s, as the demand for steam heat approached the capacity of these plants, the company decided to replace them with a single central plant.

Construction began on Kneeland Street in 1929, and the plant went into operation on October 26, 1930. Designed by Bigelow, Wadsworth,

Hubbard & Smith, the plant rises 125 feet above the street. Its twin 250-foot stacks are a landmark for motorists on the Southeast Expressway and the Massachusetts Turnpike.

Planned to house six boilers, each with a steaming capacity of 250,000 pounds per hour, the plant was initially equipped with only two, fired at first by pulverized coal but converted to oil in 1961. The station was designed ultimately to provide 1.25 million pounds of steam per hour to the distribution mains—equivalent, the company wrote about 1930, to the steam required to heat 100 buildings the size of the new United Shoe Machinery Building (140 Federal Street). Today the plant has four boilers with a capacity of 1.18 million pounds and, with the Minot Street Station (**552**) and a newer facility near the Prudential Center, supplies approximately 22 miles of steam mains and some 400 customers. Among the plant's more visible products is the steam that pours from the spout of a giant kettle used as part of a signpost by a restaurant near City Hall Plaza.

555   Boston Light

HULL

Little Brewster Island, Boston Harbor ^{3}44210.^{46}87700

By the early 18th century Boston had become the principal port of trade in the English colonies in North America. In 1713 Boston merchants petitioned the local colonial government, the Massachusetts General Court, for a lighthouse "on some Head Land at the Entrance of the Harbor of Boston." The conical stone lighthouse, completed in September 1716, was the earliest lighthouse in the country.

The original lighthouse was blown up when the British evacuated the city in June 1776. The present light, a conical granite tower originally 75 feet in height, was erected in 1783 at the order of the state legislature and was turned over to the federal government in 1790 (figure 13). It was here and at Cape Ann that Winslow Lewis successfully demonstrated his Argand lamp–parabolic reflector system in 1810, thereby persuading the Treasury Department to adopt the light for all the nation's lighthouses. The use of Lewis's system effectively postponed the introduction of the modern Fresnel lens for several decades.

In 1859, 14 feet were added to the tower's height, placing the top of the lantern 89 feet above ground. The present first-order Fresnel lens produces a light rated at 2 million candlepower. The light was named a National Historic Landmark by the U.S. Department of the Interior in 1966.

556   Long Island Head Light

HULL

Long Island, Boston Harbor ^{3}38650.^{46}88070

Boston Light marked the entrance to Nantasket Roads, the earliest shipping lanes into Boston. The establishment of a light on Long Island Head in 1819 signaled the adoption of a new route into Boston Harbor, via Broad Sound and President Roads.

In 1818 a committee of the Boston Marine Society noted that more vessels were entering and leaving Boston Harbor through the Broad Sound Channel than through the "Lighthouse Channel," and that with a light to guide the vessels, an even greater proportion might use the former channel. Evidently much of the traffic to and from the Maine coast was using this route, and the committee made note of the petition of the Portland Marine Society for a light on Long Island Head. Congress appears to have acted with some speed on the request. In March 1819 the Collector of the Port of Boston requested a committee of the Boston Marine Society to designate a suitable site for a lighthouse on Long Island Head, and by October of the same year the lamps on the new beacon had been lit.

The brick tower was moved to its present location in 1900 when Fort Strong (**558**) was expanded. The tower is one of 43 surviving lighthouses in the state. The only brick lighthouse of greater age is the Annisquam Harbor Light built in Gloucester in 1801. The light was abandoned about 1981, and today its chief navigational function is as a daymark.

557   Fort Warren

HULL

Georges Island, Boston Harbor ^{3}41000.^{46}87000

Located on Georges Island at the entrance to Boston Harbor, Fort Warren was the principal fortification in Boston Harbor between its completion in 1863 and its final abandonment after World War II. The fort is also considered the most important engineering work of Sylvanus Thayer (1785–1872), who from 1833 to 1863 was in charge of the construction of fortifications in Boston Harbor and of the improvement of harbors along the New England coast.

Construction of the fort was begun in 1834 and was not completed for 29 years. The post was a bastioned star fort, built mostly of Quincy granite. Its outer walls (eight feet thick and 600 to 660 feet in length) enclosed a parade ground of some four acres. Casement guns (thirty

32 pounders) protected the principal front, while howitzers armed the bastions. The main sally port was through Front No. 3 (facing northwest), entered over a bridge from the coverface.

Fort Warren underwent notable periods of modernization in the 1870s and again in the 1890s, when modern armaments were installed. Several structures date from the early 20th century, including a power plant, a two-story brick hospital, and a mine storage building.

In 1958 the United States deeded Fort Warren to the Metropolitan District Commission, which since that time has administered the fort as a historic site. The MDC also maintains a small marina on the island.

558   Fort Strong

HULL

Long Island, Boston Harbor ^{3}38800.^{46}88100

Fort Strong, first established on Noddles Island (East Boston) during the Civil War, was named in honor of General George C. Strong, who was killed at the siege of Fort Wagner in 1863. The fort was moved to Long Island Head in 1867, where, like the light, it controlled the channel between Long and Deer islands.

The fort was extensively enlarged in 1899 with batteries of six- and twelve-inch guns. Its facilities had become obsolete by the time of World War II, during which it was used as a mine operations center. The post was closed at the end of the war. Today missile silos constructed during the 1950s provide temporary overflow storage for Boston City Hospital Records.

559   Fort Standish

HULL

Lovell's Island, Boston Harbor ^{3}41100.^{46}88000

Fort Standish was established by the War Department soon after 1900 as part of a chain of new fortifications, including forts Heath and Banks in Winthrop and, in Hull, Fort Andrews on Peddock's Island and Fort Revere on Nantasket Head.

This series of forts was among the first to install the "disappearing gun carriage" that had been introduced experimentally by the English in 1885. In this system a gun's recoil energy is captured and used to return the gun to a protected position behind an earthwork after firing and to raise the gun to a firing position once it has been reloaded.

Unlike the earlier forts at Long and Georges islands, Fort Standish on Lovells Island could control both shipping lanes: Nantasket Roads and President Roads. It was only after World War II thst the army completely abandoned the concept of harbor defence by long-range artillery. Fort Standish was turned over to the Metropolitan District Commission in 1951. Today approximately 22 campsites share the island with the concrete remains of the fort.

560   Graves Light

NANTASKET BEACH

The Graves, Boston Harbor ^{3}46040.^{46}91780

Boston Harbor's outermost light is Graves Light, built by the U.S. Lighthouse Board in 1903–1905 on Graves Ledge. The Graves is a rocky outcrop on the southeast side of the Broad Sound's south channel. It had been marked by a bell buoy since the 1850s. Between 1892 and 1905 the Army Corps of Engineers dredged the south channel to a depth of 30 feet, and with this improvement to the channel a better marker was required.

Construction was begun on the 113-foot tower in June 1903. Royal Luther of Malden, the builder, constructed the light of Cape Ann granite. The light was originally equipped with a 380,000-candlepower lamp. The original (French) hyperradiant lens was replaced in 1975 and is now on display at the National Museum of American History, in the exhibition "1876." Today the automated beacon has a nominal range of 24 miles.

The location was named for Thomas Graves, Vice Admiral of John Winthrop's fleet when it sailed to New England in 1629.

561   Metropolitan Sewerage Board: Deer Island Pumping Station

HULL

Deer Island, Boston Harbor ^{3}38600.^{46}90160

The act of 1889 establishing the Metropolitan Sewerage Commission was the earliest of several important pieces of state legislation recognizing the interdependent requirements of the communities in the Boston metropolitan area. Boston had completed its own sewage disposal system in 1883 (**000**) and, to protect the Mystic River water supply, had constructed the Mystic Valley Sewer in 1878. The Metropolitan Sewerage Act of 1889, written by the State Board of Health, called for the creation of a North Metropolitan Sewerage System to collect the wastes of communities between Woburn and Winthrop. Chief engineer for the system in both its design and construction phases was Howard A. Carson, who later became chief engineer of the Boston Transit Commission (**534**). Three pumping stations—at Charlestown (**000**), East Boston (**000**), and Deer Island—would pump the effluent to an outfall beyond Deer Island, where it would be carried to sea. The Deer Island Pumping Station was completed in November 1894 (figure 14). Like those at East Boston and Charlestown, it was originally equipped with two triple-expansion Corliss-type steam engines built by the Edward P. Allis Company of Milwaukee, though provision was made for a third engine to be added when necessary. Each engine drove a submerged centrifugal pump, also built by Allis, designed to pump 45 million gallons per day. The long, single-story brick pumping station was designed by Arthur F. Gray, who had done the one at East Boston; the superintendent's house was designed in the office of Ernest N. Boyden. The engines were replaced with diesel equipment in the 1950s, and pumping was discontinued altogether in 1968 after the completion of the Deer Island treatment plant nearby. The building is currently empty.

Notes

Abbreviations

NR: National Register of Historic Places.

NRp: National Register designation pending.

HAER or HABS: Recorded with measured drawings and/or photographs by the Historic American Engineering Record or the Historic American Buildings Survey, National Park Service, Washington, D.C.

Stone: Orra Stone, *History of Massachusetts Industries*, 4 vols. (Boston: S. J. Clarke, 1930).

NCAB: *National Cyclopedia of American Biography*, 60 + vols. (New York: James T. White, 1898–1981).

PIHSC: *Professional & Industrial History of Suffolk County*, 3 vols. (Boston: Boston History Co., 1894).

BET: *Boston Evening Transcript*.

Barlow: Insurance survey prepared by Barlow's Insurance Surveys of New York City. Unless otherwise noted, all surveys are in the collection of the Manuscripts & Archives Department, Baker Library, Graduate School of Business Administration, Harvard University.

R. G. Dun: Records of R. G. Dun & Company (Massachusetts volumes), collection of the Manuscripts & Archives Department, Baker Library, as above.

Boston Proper   Walter Muir Whitehill, *Boston, A Topographical History* (Cambridge: Harvard University Press, 1968); see also "Boston" entries in Committee for a New England Bibliography, *Massachusetts: A Bibliography of Its History* (Boston: G. K. Hall, 1976), pp. 116–206.

501   NR ("Blackstone Block"); Edward G. Porter, *Rambles in Old Boston, New England* (Boston: Cupples, Upham, 1887), pp. 31–48; Samuel Adams Drake, *Old Landmarks and Historic Personages of Boston* (Boston: James R. Osgood, 1874), pp. 143–144.

502   "John S. Paine," *Boston Herald* 21 April 1903, p. 12; *Boston and Its Points of Interest* (Boston, 1893), p. 350; Edward S. Cooke, "The Boston Furniture Industry in 1880," *Old-Time New England* 70(1980):92–93; Paine Furniture Company, *One Hundred Years at Paine's, 1835–1935* (Boston: Paine Furniture Co., 1935). Drawings for a Paine & Shearer building of the same proportions are in the Preston Collection of the Boston Public Library's Fine Arts Department.

503   *Boston Globe* 21 February 1913, p. 1.

504   NR ("Fulton–Commercial Streets District"); "George T. McLauthlin," *PIHSC* 3:646–650; "Martin B. McLauthlin," *NCAB* 34(1948):59.

505   NR ("Custom House District"); Mickail Koch for Boston Landmarks Commission; "Calvin A. Richards," in Edwin M. Bacon, ed., *Boston of To-Day* (Boston: Post Publishing Company, 1892), pp. 367–368.

506   NR ("Newspaper Row"); "Daniel D. Badger," *New York Times* 19 November 1884, p. 2; Pamela Fox for the Boston Landmarks Commission; *Boston Post* 31 August 1874, p. 1.

507   NRp ("Commercial Palace District"); Pamela Fox for the Boston Landmarks Commission.

508   NRp ("Commercial Palace District"); "Jacob Sleeper," *BET* 1 April 1889, p. 4; "George W. Pope," *BET* 17 January 1896, p. 10; *Boston Journal* 17 January 1896, p. 2; Pamela Fox for Boston Landmarks Commission.

510   *Leading Manufacturers and Merchants of the City of Boston* (Boston: International Publishing Co., 1885), p. 140; "John Wilkins Carter," *NCAB* 40(1955):49–50; "Theodore Minot Clark," *NCAB* 30(1943):226.

511   NR ("Custom House District"); William G. Preston Drawing Collection, Fine Arts Dept., Boston Public Library; George L. Gould, *Historical Sketch of the Paint, Oil, Varnish and Allied Trades of Boston* (Boston: privately printed, 1915), pp. 88–91; Charles Stanhope Damrell, *A Half Century of Boston's Building* (Boston: L. P. Hager, 1895), opp. p. 204; *Leading Manufacturers and Merchants of the City of Boston* (1885), p. 186.

512   NR ("Boston Common and Public Garden"); "Bronze Tablet Placed on Public Garden Footbridge," *Journal of the Boston Society of Civil Engineers* 23(1936):240–241.

513   NR; "Frederick L. Ames," *NCAB* 14(1910):202–203; "The New Ames Building," *The Boston Daily Globe,* 2 July 1889, p. 8.

514   NR; *Inland Architect & News Record* 22(October 1893):31; Damrell, p. 70; Carl W. Condit, *American Building Art: The Nineteenth Century* (New York: Oxford University Press, 1960), p. 72; on Z-bar columns see Corydon T. Purdy, "The Steel Skeleton Type of High Buildings," *Engineering News* 26(12 December 1891):560.

515   NR ("Theatre Multiple Resource Area"); E. S. Mansfield, "The Edison System in Boston—Its Development and Present Status," *Electrical World & Engineer* 37(18 May 1901):797–822; D. S., "Origins of the Boston Edison Company, 1885–1887," unattributed Boston University thesis, collection of Vaughn Zulalian, Boston Edison Company; "Charles Leavitt Edgar," *NCAB* 27(1939):144–145.

516   Mansfield, pp. 797–822; "The Power Plants Which Light Boston," *The Engineer* (Cleveland) 39(1 September 1902):589–594; "Expansion of the Boston Edison System." *Electrical World & Engineer* 43(21 May 1904):950.

517   "Joseph F. Paul," *BET* 30 January 1889, p. 4; Whitehill, pp. 119–140; R. G. Dun (Joseph F. Paul & Co., Bay State Organ Co.). Preston's elaborate drawings for the 1872 mill are now in the Fine Arts Department of the Boston Public Library.

518   "John J. McNutt," *BET* 15 June 1894, p. 8; "Sketch," *Boston Globe* 13 April 1916, p. 16; Edwin M. Bacon, ed., *Boston of To-Day* (Boston: Post Publishing Company, 1892), p. 310.

519   "William F. Badger," *Boston Daily Globe* 12 August 1897, p. 2.

520   NR ("South End Historic District"); "Joseph F. Pray," *BET* 12 March 1904, p. 17; R. G. Dun (Thomas Goddard, Joseph F. Pray, J. T. Gurney).

521   "Gideon F. T. Reed," *BET* 4 March 1892, p. 5; Barlow #8747.

522   "John C. Reece," *BET* 2 April 1896, p. 5; Stone, pp. 1163, 1459; *Boston and Its Points of Interest* (Boston, 1893), p. 298; *Fifty Years of Boston* (Boston: Boston Tercentenary Committee, 1932), p. 172.

523 "Charles Goodyear," *BET* 23 May 1896, p. 9; "Christian Dancel," *BET* 14 October 1898, p. 10; "S. W. Winslow," *NCAB* 15(1916):196–197: Stone, pp. 1165–1168.
524 Stone, p. 1589.
525 NR ("South End Historic District"); the building is minutely described in "The Manufacture of Pianofortes, Chickering & Co.," *Frank Leslie's Illustrated Newspaper* 7(16 April 1859):305–309. See also J. Parton, "The Piano in the United States," *Atlantic Monthly* 20(July 1867):82–98; *PIHSC* 3:436–441; Nancy A. Smith, "Pianoforte Manufacturing in Nineteenth-Century Boston," *Old-Time New England* 69(Summer–Fall 1978):37–47; Barlow #6400; Stone, pp. 1283–1287.
526 NR ("South End Historic District"); *PIHSC* 3:444; Stone, pp. 1447–1448; *Leading Manufacturers and Merchants of the City of Boston* (1885), p. 171; Barlow #5101; Daniel Spillane, *History of the American Pianoforte* (New York: D. Spillane, 1890), pp. 305–307.
528 Barlow #5088; R. G. Dun.
529 Alfred Dolge, *Pianos and their Makers* (Covina, CA: Covina Publishing, 1911), pp. 53–57; R. G. Dun; "Charles Henry Bacon," *BET* 12 December 1906, p. 7; "B. F. Baker," *NCAB* 7(1897):429–430.
530 Dolge, pp. 292–293; Barlow #7490; R. G. Dun. There is a large lithograph of Emerson's 1866 factory on Albany Street in the collection of the Boston Athenaeum.
531 *Boston and Its Points of Interest* (Boston, 1893), pp. 92–93; *PIHSC* 3:443; Damrell, p. 80; "A. S. Drisko," Edwin M. Bacon, ed., *Boston of To-Day* (Boston: Post Publishing Co., 1892), p. 215.
532 Dolge, pp. 337–338; Smith, pp. 37–47.
533 "Frederick S. Pearson," *NCAB* 18(1922):123–124; "Work on the West End Station," *Electrical Engineer* 10(15 October 1890):407–408; "Central Power Station," *The Street Railway Journal* 8(September 1892):516–519; Damrell, p. 485 ("largest and most complete system").
534 NR; Brian J. Cudahy, *Change at Park Street Under* (Brattleboro, VT: Stephen Greene Press, 1976); Boston Street Railway Assn., *Rapid Transit Lines in Boston, Bulletin No. 5* (Cambridge: BSRA, 1964), 58–64; Boston Elevated Railway Co., *Fifty Years of Unified Transportation in Metropolitan Boston* (Boston: BER, 1938); "The Boston Electric Railway Subway," *Electrical Engineer* 19(12 June 1895):532–534; Francis Ward Chandler, ed., *Municipal Architecture in Boston, from Designs by Edmund M. Weelwright* (Boston: Bates & Guild, 1898), pp. 50–52; Annual Reports of the Boston Transit Commission for the years 1894–1898.
535 Laurence B. Manley, "The Stations of the Washington Street Tunnel," *Engineering News* 62(7 October 1909):367–371; John S. Hodgson, "Washington Street Tunnel, Boston," *Railroad Age Gazette* 45(27 November 1908):1435–1439; *Rapid Transit Lines in Boston*, pp. 78–79.
536 J. A. Stewart, "The New Street Railway Tunnel Under Boston Harbor," *Scientific American* 84(23 March 1901):185–186; "The East Boston Tunnel," *Railroad Gazette* 35(10 April 1903):259–261; "Construction of the East Boston Tunnel," *Engineering Record* 7(14 November 1903):552–554, 585–587; Boston Street Railway Association, Inc., *Rapid Transit Lines in Boston* (Cambridge: BSRA, 1964), pp. 86–87; Boston Elevated Railway, *Fifty Years of Unified Transportation in Metropolitan Boston* (Boston: BER, 1938), pp. 60–62, 94–95.
537 Wilbur W. Davis, "The Beacon Hill Subway Tunnel in Boston," *Engineering Record* 66(13 July 1912):32–36; "Methods of Constructing the Beacon Hill Rapid Transit Tunnel," *Engineering & Contracting* 37(22 May 1912):571–572.
538 NR; HAER; Carroll L. V. Meeks, *The Railroad Station, An Architectural History* (New Haven: Yale University Press, 1956), p. 121 et seq.

539   "The Lincoln Power Station," *Engineering Record* 44(17 August 1901):147–151; "Power Plant Extensions," *Electrical World* 53(18 February 1909):445–448; "New Power Station and Elevated Railway System," *Street Railway Journal* 17(2 March 1901):253–259.

540   "Walter M. Lowney," *BET* 5 April 1923, p. 6; Stone, pp. 1461–1462; "Steam Plant of the Lowney Chocolate Factory," *Engineering Record* 38(2 July 1898):101–102.

541   Stone, p. 1627.

542   "George F. Schrafft," *NCAB* 26(1937):411.

543   "Jacob L. Loose," *NCAB* 19(1926):34; Stone, pp. 1311–1312.

545   Stone, p. 1626, and vol. 4, pp. 213–214; "Prince—the Palatable Pasta...," *Industry* 48(October 1983):33–34; Mass. Dept. of Community Affairs, *Built to Last* (Washington, D.C.: The Preservation Press, 1977), pp. 56–57.

546–550   Interviews with Vaughn Zulalian, Manager of Electrical Operations, Boston Edison.

548   NRp ("Commercial Palace District"); "Electric Distributing Station, Boston, Mass.," *The American Architect* 117(26 May 1920):653.

551   "B. & M. Opens First Unit of New Passenger Station at Boston," *Railway Age* 85(25 August 1928):337–341; Frank C. Shepherd, "Recent Terminal Improvements of the Boston & Maine Railroad," *Journal of the Boston Society of Civil Engineers* 17(1930):1–28.

552   Personal correspondence with Paul Johnson and Robert Kelly, Boston Edison; "Electric Light & Power Station, Boston & Maine Railroad," *Engineering Record* 30(2 June 1894):9–11; *Steam Heating Service, Its Development and Application in Boston* (Boston: Edison Electric Illuminating Company, c. 1931), pp. 5–9.

553   "Rare Old Bridges Replaced in B. & M. Railroad Terminal Improvements at Boston," *Engineering News-Record* 107(5 November 1931):718–722; "Boston & Maine Completes Large Terminal Project at Boston," *Railway Age* 92(5 March 1932):390–395; Carl W. Condit, *American Building Art: the Nineteenth Century* (New York: Oxford University Press, 1960), pp. 101–102; 1961 date courtesy of Edward Levay, Boston & Maine Railroad.

554   P. W. Swain, "Simplicity is the Keynote of Boston's Kneeland Street Heating Plant," *Power* 73(27 January 1931):134–137; *Steam Heating Service, Its Development and Application in Boston* (Boston: Edison Electric Illuminating Company, c. 1931).

555   NR; Francis Ross Holland, Jr., *America's Lighthouses: Their Illustrated History Since 1716* (Brattleboro, VT: Stephen Greene Press, 1972), pp. 8–10, 14–15.

556   NRp; William A. Baker, *A History of the Boston Marine Society* (Boston: Boston Marine Society, 1968), pp. 129–130; Leslie L. Fox et al., National Register nomination, "Lighthouses of Massachusetts: Thematic Group," Massachusetts Historical Commission.

557   NR; Aubrey Parkman, *Army Engineers in New England* (Waltham: U.S. Army Corps of Engineers, New England Division, 1978), p. 19ff.

558   Emily & David Kales, *All About the Boston Harbor Islands* (Boston: Herman Publishing, 1976), p. 72.

559   Parkman, pp. 112–120; G. H. Powell, "Disappearing Gun Carriages in the United States," *Engineering Magazine* 19(June 1900):411–418; Kales, pp. 52–53.

560   NRp; Baker, pp. 250–251; Kales, p. 43; Fox and Salzman, "Lighthouses of Massachusetts."

561   Metropolitan Sewerage Commission, *Sixth Annual Report for the Year Ending Sept. 30th, 1894* (Boston: Wright & Potter, 1895); *Seventh Annual Report for the Year Ending Sept. 30, 1895* (Boston: Wright & Potter, 1896); "The Metropolitan Sewerage Systems of Massachusetts," *Engineering News* 31(25 January 1894): 62–63; "Deer Island Sewerage Works," *Engineering Record* 31(9 January 1895):188–190.

Industrial Classification Index

The Industrial Classification Index was developed by the Historic American Engineering Record in 1973 to provide a means of organizing historic industrial and engineering structures into standard categories. The classification is derived primarily from the Standard Industrial Classification Manual (known as the SIC Manual) published by the U.S. Department of Commerce. As modified to meet the needs of industrial archeology, the classification includes ten categories, as follows.

I. Extractive Industries

II. Bulk Product Industries

Chemical Industry

Paints and varnishes: 501, 510

Food Processing

Dairy and bakery products: 543, 545

Confectionery: 540, 541, 542, 544

Primary Metal Industries

Nonferrous foundries: 511

Lumber, Timber and Paper Industries

Millwork, veneer, etc.: 517, 518, 519, 527

Furniture: 502

III. Manufacturing Industries

Machinery Manufacture

Engines, pumps, and turbines: 504

Textile machinery: 522

Materials-handling equipment (elevators): 504

Other (shoe machinery): 523

Fabricated Metal Products

Plumbing materials: 503

Transportation Equipment

Carriages and wagons: 520

Street Index